VIV RICHARDS
THE AUTHORISED BIOGRAPHY

VIV RICHARDS
THE AUTHORISED BIOGRAPHY

Trevor McDonald

PELHAM BOOKS
London

For Lawson, who knows about the struggle more than most.
And Tim, that he one day will.

First published in Great Britain by
Pelham Books Ltd
44 Bedford Square
London WC1B 3DU
June 1984
Reprinted July 1984
Reprinted September 1984

British Library Cataloguing in Publication Data

McDonald, Trevor
  Viv Richards.
  1. Richards, Viv   2. Cricket players——
  Biography
  I. Title
  796.3'08'0924   GV915.R4/

ISBN 0 7207 1512 1

Printed and bound in Great Britain by
Butler & tanner, Frome, Somerset

ACKNOWLEDGEMENTS

Writing a book about Viv Richards has been made a distinctly pleasurable task by the number of players only too willing to talk about the West Indian batsman. I have benefited from their many stories and I am greatly indebted to them.

It would be impossible to mention all those players who helped, but Pat Pocock of Surrey was generous in sharing his experiences of playing against Richards, and the Somerset opening batsman Peter Roebuck not only gave permission for the use of his book *Slices of Cricket* as a reference, but also pointed me in the right direction in my attempt to understand Richards the player and the man. Colin Atkinson of Somerset offered his assistance with typical warmth, and no one could write anything about Somerset without the help of 'Jock' McCoombe.

In India with the West Indies on tour I was made to feel one of the party by the manager Wes Hall, the captain Clive Lloyd and by Gordon Greenidge and Andy Roberts. All the other West Indian players willingly assisted in the project.

I drew heavily on *Wisden* and I am particularly grateful to its editor John Woodcock. The Secretary at Kennington Oval, Ian Scott Browne, was unfailingly kind in allowing use of his library for my research.

C.L.R. James, the great West Indian philosopher and writer, and his book *Beyond the Boundary* were more than an inspiration. They were my guiding light. And I am grateful to the poet Eddie Braithwaite for allowing me to make use of his poetry in attempting to 'explain' the West Indian approach to the game.

Throughout the writing of the book, I avidly read the reports of former colleagues, like Michael Melford of the *Daily Telegraph*. This book could not have been written without these.

My special thanks must go to Rebekah Ponsford who undertook the typing of the manuscript and to Abigail Larter for her patience and understanding as editor.

Theirs was the invaluable help. Any errors in fact or perception are mine.

What do they know of cricket, who only cricket know

C. L. R. James

Vivian Richards, one of the two Antiguans in the West Indies side, remains the world's most brilliant batsman. Sir Gary Sobers was the last powerful single influence on the game; before that Sir Donald Bradman was

Wisden 1981

With Viv during a lunch interval in Bombay

INTRODUCTION

*To envisage circumstance
all calm,
That is the top of sovereignty*

Keats

Books written by admirers of their subject are at best predictable, at worst unreliable. And since from the first time I saw him bat I became an unashamed convert to the Viv Richards school of cricket, honesty dictated that I declare the fact.

In the eight years I have known him, nothing about the man or his game has diminished my admiration. If anything, it has grown.

I would like to think that I brought to the task of writing this biography some journalistic skill, a genuine love for the game and an abiding interest in what I have come to regard as the 'sociology' of West Indian cricket. That interest has been part of my experience, a large slice of my life.

Like Viv Richards, I was born in the West Indies,

*sound of the sea
came in at my window,
life heaved and breathed in me then
with the strength of that turbulent soil.*

My unremarkable attempts at coming to grips with the most elementary principles of the game foundered in the same atmosphere and on those same early West Indian wickets of my youth on which the genius of Viv Richards later flowered.

Many years before I began broadcasting cricket in the West Indies, and covering tours in England and Australia, my experiences had taught me that West Indian cricket is unlike any other. Three powerful influences shaped its development and ensured its standing in society.

The first was obvious: West Indian success on cricket fields abroad, particularly in England, turned cricket from an enjoyable pastime into a positive expression of burgeoning West Indian nationalism. West Indians were discovering that although, in the brutal parlance of that colonial age, they were the 'hewers of wood and drawers of water' for the metropolitan powers, in cricket they were good enough to compete with their political masters on even terms.

The second factor, arising from the first, had to do with the beginning of the movement in the West Indies to political self-determination. This gave West Indian cricket a vibrant nationalistic pride. It was a crucial factor in the emergence of a long line of West Indian players, including Viv Richards.

The third was unlikely. The poetic cadences of John Arlott's cricket commentaries on the World Service of the BBC had a profound influence on West Indian cricket and those who followed the game. He gave cricket an identity, which was neither Oxbridge nor that of the Establishment. West Indians saw Arlott's language as part of a third world proletarian revolution, which they were happy to join with zeal. Arlott's commentaries, with neither bias nor patronage, became a part of everyday West Indian life.

There are West Indians who recall to this day Arlott's commentary during the historic 1950 West Indies tour of England. As the 'three Ws' reduced the English bowling to pulp, he said: 'This is not cricket, it's civilised murder.'

And when, 13 years later, Frank Worrell led the West Indies in England for the first time, John Arlott, quoting a famous English umpire, intoned at the end of a riveting day's play: 'And that, gentlemen, concludes the entertainment for the day.'

West Indians too had always seen cricket as entertainment, an expression in sport of the natural exuberance of West Indian life. So they embraced Arlott's words as part of the 'new language' of cricket.

Viv Richards is not only the best batsman in the world, he is also the most entertaining.

It is not often remembered that Richards in effect replaced Gary Sobers in the West Indies batting line-up. I have never heard him refer to that fact, nor would he be drawn on his friend Ian Botham's description of him as a better player than Don Bradman. Richards is too modest. That is fitting. Great cricketers, like great statesmen or great nations, have never been boasters or buffoons, but perceivers of the perils of their profession, who manned themselves to face those perils.

Watching Richards bat in a match against Surrey at Taunton one day, I was brought into a conversation about whether it was ever possible to check the rate at which runs flow from the broad bat of the 'King of Taunton' when he's in rampant mood. An enthusiastic Surrey player suggested with fervour that even Richards could be tamed, if fields were properly set and bowlers bowled to them. The Surrey manager, older and wiser, agreed with the general statement in principle, but averred that in practice Richards would find gaps even in the most carefully set field.

The course of the discussion ebbed and flowed. All the while a former Somerset player and county umpire – and an avowed Richards fan – listened with a mischievous indulgent smile. He had just begun to explain why it was almost impossible to tame Richards when he was on good form, when the West Indian number three lifted one of the Surrey bowlers high into the pavilion and then promptly drove the two succeeding deliveries through the offside for four.

That ended the discussion.

Last season Richards missed a number of games through injury, and although by mid-August he was way ahead in the Schweppes County Championship batting averages (90.45), he still had not reached 1,000 runs for the season, even though about a dozen other players had. It was most unusual for him not to be comfortably ahead in the number of runs scored.

One of his best innings was against Leicestershire in mid-July. He opened the batting for Somerset and stayed to make 216 before he fell to Andy Roberts, his old sparring partner and fellow Antiguan.

Two weeks later he scored an undefeated 117 in his team's score of 337 for 7.

He got a fine century against Kent at Taunton at the beginning of September and although Ian Botham was the man who played a wonderfully mature innings to ensure Somerset's place in the Nat West Trophy final at Lords, Richards' half-century was the highlight of his team's first-innings tally of 193, which in the end was just too much for Kent.

I first interviewed Richards after his memorable double century against England at the Oval in 1976. I asked him about an incredible shot he'd played off the bowling of Derek Underwood. Facing a ball, not all that short, Richards had gone on to the back foot and hit Underwood over the long Oval extra-cover boundary for six. He smiled and said:

'The ball was there to be hit and I put everything into the shot. I decided to have a go because I saw the ball very early.'

Seeing the ball early has been one of his greatest assets. His shoulders and wrists are also formidably strong.

His batting can be so outrageously audacious, that he always offers a sporting chance to the persistent bowler. He is exciting because he is fallible. His heart is set not solely on the accumulation of large scores; his instincts are not for the gladiatorial kill, but for the glories and the thrill of combat.

Richards' temper occasionally gets the better of him and there is a rebellious side to his nature. He was not in England at the time, but he would have applauded Ian Botham's decision to defy the Test and County Cricket Board and risk injury by playing football for Scunthorpe only a few days before he was due to leave for Fiji, New Zealand and Pakistan with an England touring party. Richards and Botham are much more than just good friends – they are soul mates.

Alf Gover, that wise and kindly gentleman of English cricket coaching, told me how many years before the Richards legend was born, he was asked to 'have a look at Viv and give him a little help in learning to adapt to English conditions'.

One Saturday morning Gover, who'd been told about the exciting Antiguan prospect, asked his best slow bowler, an Australian left-armer, to bowl at Viv. Gover recalls that the first ball was a well-flighted 'chinaman', the left-hander's 'wrong un'. Richards spotted it with the greatest of ease and had more than enough time to play an unhurried shot. Gover was impressed from that moment. He felt that Richards was 'in a different class to other players. He moved well, was quiet within himself, and everything he did he did with great dignity.'

That's the Viv Richards I know and the player I have so enjoyed writing about.

At the time of writing, it is by no means certain that Viv Richards will succeed Clive Lloyd as captain of the West Indies team. At a team dinner at the conclusion of the 1983 Prudential World Cup, Lloyd was mildly rebuked by the West Indies team manager, Clyde Walcott, for suggesting that he (Lloyd) would hand over the cap-

OPPOSITE One of Richards' greatest assets is his ability to pounce on the short ball. During the 1981 England tour of the West Indies the Yorkshire and England wicket keeper David Bairstow recognises the need for evasive action (*Adrian Murrell*)

5

taincy to Richards in a year's time. Walcott sternly reminded Lloyd that the captaincy of the team was not to be given as a gift by any incumbent. Richards heard this exchange and is aware that he may not be the only player in the running to lead the West Indies.

If the captaincy were to be given to either Gordon Greenidge or Jeffrey Dujon, it would be a grievous wound to Richards' pride. But it would not be fatal; he would swallow his hurt and tell himself that perhaps it was not ordained that he should be the West Indies captain. And he would redouble his efforts to make runs for his team. That is the Richards way. He is a player and a man who, whatever the controversies or problems of his time, retains that visible dignity and inner calm which the poet Keats described as 'the top of sovereignty'.

CHAPTER ONE

We will make (the West Indies) grovel

Tony Greig

Nobody talks to Viv Richards like that

Viv Richards

It's not in the nature of Isaac Vivian Alexander Richards to speak of himself in the third person. By no stretch of the imagination could he be described as an arrogant man. Yet, in a strange way, he is able to detach his own personality from the talent which, by common consent, has made him the greatest batsman in the game today.

Richards is serious about that talent; and he is fiercely proud of it.

He comes very close to believing that it's God-given and that he was charged with the responsibility of using it to its best advantage. That makes him humble. But he is not in the least apologetic about the fact that he can see the cricket ball and pick up its line earlier than any other living batsman.

That gives him time to play his shots. It's the key to the confident, uninhibited manner in which he plays, and the glorious freedom with which he strokes the ball.

His approach – a combination of humility, seriousness and burning pride – was shaped by the class structure which has always dominated the West Indian game and nurtured by the politics of contemporary cricket. That's why, on the eve of that first test between England and the West Indies in 1976, the England captain, Tony Greig, touched a raw nerve with his 'grovel' remark. And not only with Viv Richards.

Three years before the 1976 series, England had been overwhelmed by a powerful West Indies side. Richards had not been a member of that side, but England lost all three test matches played, and on 27 August at Lords the West Indies won by an innings and 226 runs, their biggest-ever margin of victory over England.

In 1976 West Indian cricket seemed on the crest of that same wave. And the team for the first test at Trent Bridge looked a strong

well-rounded side. On paper, the batting appeared formidable. Roy Fredericks and Gordon Greenidge were numbers one and two. Fredericks, the little Guyanese player, combined a solid defence with a wonderful attacking style and his partner, Greenidge, who'd made a hundred in his first test appearance in India two years earlier, had quickly established himself as a reliable opening batsman, who was at the same time one of the hardest hitters. In savaging a Sussex attack in the 1975 English County season, Greenidge had struck 13 towering sixes on his way to amassing 259 runs for Hampshire.

Number three in the batting line-up was Vivian Richards. He'd made his test debut in that same Bangalore test as did Greenidge and was being widely talked about as a batsman of the greatest promise. The rest of the batting order read: Alvin Kallicharan, Clive Lloyd, Bernard Julien, Larry Gomes and Deryck Murray.

Nor was the West Indian bowling for that first test at Nottingham to be written off. A mild attack of glandular fever had kept Michael Holding out of the reckoning for the first test, but Wayne Daniel's raw hostility was an excellent replacement. The attack was spearheaded by Andy Roberts and supported by Vanburn Holder and the left-handed Julien.

By contrast to the settled appearance of the touring side, there was an odd look about the England team. England were, once again, a team on the brink of transition, and, not for the first time, the England selectors hadn't quite decided which way to jump.

The England captain was the ebullient Tony Greig. Much later, during the traumatic upheaval of the Kerry Packer Affair, a distinguished cricket correspondent was to attribute what he saw as Tony Greig's 'treachery' in persuading other players to 'defect' to the 'circus' to the fact that Greig was 'English only by adoption, which is not the same as being English through and through'. In the summer of 1976, though, England needed Greig.

He'd been appointed captain after the painful demise the previous summer of Mike Denness. Poor Denness had meekly put the Australians in to bat, after winning the toss in the first test; there'd been a terrific thunderstorm on the second day, England's batting collapsed twice and the Australians took a stranglehold on the series.

OPPOSITE The Hampshire and West Indies opening batsman Gordon Greenidge has often provided the solid base from which Richards could proceed to build a West Indies innings (ASP)

Denness had been made to take the blame, and he paid the penalty. Greig brought to the England captaincy that outward show of aggression which his predecessor lacked. With it though, went an exuberance so extravagant at times that it appalled even his most committed supporters.

Perhaps it was the supreme confidence of Tony Greig that led the England selectors to hedge their bets for the first test against the West Indies. They doubtless reasoned that against a solid-looking West Indies team, some tried and tested experience was an urgent requirement. So the England selectors did an extraordinary thing: they recalled the famous Yorkshire allrounder and former England captain, Brian Close, at the grand old age of forty-five. Also in the England team were David Steele, whose chance to play for his country had come in the evening of his career, and John Snow, the England·fast bowler, who was also said to be 'getting on'.

Grafting the highly respected and experienced Close on to a predominantly young England team could not have been the simplest of operations, even for the England selectors. Close had been an England captain; now he'd been persuaded to play under the infinitely less experienced Greig. The styles of the two men could hardly have been more different. Greig was as stridently vocal and extrovert as Close was taciturn and private. The English cricket press had a field day.

None could doubt Close's stern determination and his legendary fighting qualities. But could a player of forty-five bring anything to the task of coping with the pace of the young West Indian tigers, save a stout heart and a sound memory? If Tony Greig had any doubts about the answer to that question, he decided, in typical fashion, to dispel them with sweeping rhetoric. Boldly proclaiming a doctrine which sounded very like a plan for the joint captaincy of the England side, he added for good measure that he and Brian Close would make the West Indies 'grovel'.

The rest of the England team was: Edrich, Brearley, Woolmer, Knott, Old, Hendrick and Underwood.

It had perhaps never occurred to Tony Greig that for the South African captain of an English team to publicly threaten to make the West Indies 'grovel' in 1976 was probably the closest any cricketer ever came to making a formal declaration of war.

In any event, that's how the West Indians read it; and that's certainly how Greig's words were perceived by the twenty-four-year-old player from Antigua, Vivian Richards.

He says:

It came as a bit of a shock really to hear what Tony Greig had said. I suppose on one level you could say that Greigy was just trying to reassure an England side that was not too good a team. But still I was taken aback. We all were. Wayne Daniel, Andy Roberts and I had gone into the room where the team meeting was about to be held. We were early and the television was on. We weren't watching, but when news about the cricket came on we all paid attention. And then we heard the 'grovel' remark. We all knew the kinda guy Tony was, you know, he always played the game hard, but always with a lot of chat also. But even so we thought he went a bit too far. Wayne didn't say much, but Andy was quite mad. I felt it was not too brilliant a thing for a South African to say about West Indian players and it made me more determined to do well.

The senior players tried to make us put the remark behind us, to forget it. But I can tell you, what Tony had said hung over that particular team meeting and I think it made us all feel that we could not afford to let the folks down.

So when the test match started, Vivian Richards went into battle wielding his bat like a broadsword.

And on the first day of that first test match at Nottingham, in the words of one correspondent: 'The graduation of Vivian Richards from student of the highest potential to master of the batting art, stuffed Tony Greig's battle cry down his throat.'

Continuing the magnificent run of form which saw him take one century against the Australians and three against the Indians in the seven months preceding the Nottingham test, Richards tore the England attack to shreds. He was undefeated at stumps on the first day with 143 to his name. When his wicket fell, at about half past two on the second day, he had accumulated 232 brilliant runs. In his seven-and-a-half-hour occupation of the wicket he'd struck four sixes and thirty-one fours. He had shared in a third wicket stand of 303 and had set his team on an irrevocable path to victory.

Describing one purple patch in Richards' innings, the cricket correspondent of the *Daily Telegraph*, Michael Melford, wrote: 'In twenty memorable minutes after lunch, he made another 36 runs which included successive fours, two hooks and a straight drive off Snow, and a superb stroke for six over mid-off, off Underwood.'

Believing in his own infallibility by this time, Richards struck another six off Underwood, the ball just clearing Hendrick at long-on. Melford takes up the story again: 'He lifted the next ball to long-off. The catcher Tony Greig was promptly mobbed by a crowd of small boys, not unnaturally excited because they'd all been a lot younger when England last took a wicket.'

Another cricket writer called Richards' display an innings of 'cultured violence'. And so it had been. A blend of seemingly outrageous flair and prudence when required. Perfectly balanced, with wrists of steel and a marvellous quickness of eye and reflex, Richards had never been hurried into making a stroke. Even when he played and missed outside the off stump, his supreme confidence gave the bowler not the slightest bit of encouragement.

Tony Greig's England team was given a brief reprieve in the second test, but only from Richards. He'd been kept in bed for a week with 'flu.

At Headingley Richards scored 66 and 38 in his two knocks, but with his first run in that test he had taken his aggregate for 1976 to 1,381, overhauling the record set in 1964 by Australia's Bobby Simpson.

Richards ended the series against England on the same high note on which he'd begun. The Oval test was dominated by the silken grace and menacing speed of fast bowler Michael Holding. On a singularly unhelpful pitch, he took 14 England wickets for 149 runs. But if Holding delivered the *coup de grâce*, the slaughter had been started by Richards. He went out to bat after Greenidge had been trapped leg before by Bob Willis for a duck, and launched into an innings which was to be of epic greatness.

Throughout the day, without mercy, he cut and drove the ball over the hard brown Oval outfield, to the most distant boundaries. Ruthless with any deliveries short of a good length, he was capable of defending stoutly when the need arose. But the unending feature of that memorable late summer's day was the sight of England fieldsmen despairingly chasing and then retrieving the ball from

OPPOSITE First day, first test match, England v West Indies Nottingham 1976. Richards graduates from student of the game to master of the batting art (ASP)

12

behind the boundary ropes, as Richards piled on the agony. To many, there were distinct echoes in Richards' batting that day of the almost mechanical brilliance of Bradman and Ponsford in the 1930s.

By stumps on the first day of that fifth test match, Richards had scored 200. He had driven the honest medium pace of Mike Selvey as though Selvey were a slow bowler. He had been always devastating on the onside. He flicked Willis to the long-leg boundary with a kind of graceful contempt. In a moment of delightful malice he struck Underwood over the long extra cover boundary for six.

His 200 runs on the first day were not to be the end of the story. He went on to make 291, before he was bowled playing a tired drive at a delivery from Tony Greig. His score of 291 on the second day included 38 fours and was the highest-ever by a West Indian batsman at the Oval. It was also the highest-ever by a West Indian in a test in England, and Richards' own highest score in test cricket.

Running out of superlatives to describe his masterly display, the London *Evening Standard*'s front-page headline screamed: 'Calypso Run Carnival.'

From the moment he passed 250, all West Indian thoughts became fixed on Gary Sobers' score of 365. To this day, Richards maintains that nothing was further from his mind:

> You can't play an innings in that way, going after a record. Every ball has to be played on its merit and concentration is important throughout. And thinking about how many runs you want to make, or about some batting record set by someone else could disturb your concentration. I was out there to bat and to stay as long as I could. I never let myself think of making 365.

With Richards gone, the West Indies declared at a massive 687 for 8, the highest score ever made by the West Indies against England. The England captain who'd vowed to make the West Indies 'grovel' should have, by that time, become a chastened man. But if lack of tact is one of Greig's failures, it's not compensated by an ability to face the awful truth: 'Provided we concentrate hard all the time and don't get ourselves out,' he opined, 'there is no reason why we shouldn't bat all day tomorrow and go on to save the match.'

It's difficult to remember whether the concentration of the England batsmen failed them in that fateful test; and it might be an insult to Michael Holding to say that the England batsmen got themselves out. Only Amiss batted well, scoring a fine double century.

14

Tony Greig himself could never get his bat down quickly enough to keep out Holding's faster ball. Holding got him for 12 in the first innings and uprooted his middle stump in the second, when Greig had scored only one run. With the failure of Greig went that of the England team. They lost the Oval test. It was England's heaviest defeat in nearly thirty years. England had managed a draw at Trent Bridge and at Lords. At Old Trafford they had gone down by the humiliatingly wide margin of 425 runs, and they had been convincingly beaten at Headingley and at the Oval.

Viv Richards was undoubtedly the man of the series. He'd topped the batting averages and his aggregate for the tour of 829 runs set a new record for the West Indies against any country (and has been exceeded only by Bradman, Hammond and Neil Harvey). To his countrymen in the Caribbean, Viv Richards' exploits on the cricket field meant far more than beating the old enemy at cricket.

The then Deputy Prime Minister of Antigua, Lester Bird, put it this way:

> The country needed a focal point, a touchstone, which could form the basis of communal unity in common cause. He (Richards) represented that touchstone: he was the embodiment of an opportunity for a whole nation to be galvanised for a single purpose. The common cause, that single purpose, became Viv Richards' success on the international cricket stage ... he personified what we perceived ourselves to be: young, dynamic and talented but yet unrecognised in the world.

Mr Bird went even further. He said: 'Richards was a stabilising force at a time when politics threatened to disrupt the very fabric and fibre of the society.' Not for the first time, a West Indian politician had found West Indian success on the cricket field a suitable metaphor for political progress in the islands themselves.

In 1962 the then Prime Minister of Trinidad and Tobago, Dr Eric Williams, was postulating the theory that there was a direct parallel between West Indian success on cricket fields abroad and the growth of the movement towards political independence and self-determination. Speaking at a political meeting and in the run-up to Trinidad's independence from Britain, he remarked on an upcoming tour of England by a team of West Indian cricketers: 'In the 1950s we went to learn, now we go to teach.'

Writing about Viv Richards' first test century against India in the

Richards sharing a moment of pride with his greatest admirer, the Prime Minister of Antigua, Lester Bird. Of Richards, Bird says: 'He personified what we perceived ourselves to be: young, dynamic and talented.' (*This picture was taken by his teammate Gordon Greenidge*)

1974/75 series, the Antiguan Deputy Prime Minister had made the following observation: 'With every boundary, we collectively felt a sense of pride, of achievement and of togetherness.'

Regional pride, fuelled by political change, had become part of the growing strength of the West Indian game. That pride had begun with the appointment of Frank Magdelene Worrell as West Indian captain in the early 1960s. He was the first black man to be made captain of a West Indies team. With Worrell's captaincy, the West Indies and West Indian cricket changed irrevocably. A new age had begun, an age of greater self-confidence, an age of national spirit.

Viv Richards is much too young to have seen Frank Worrell in action. He had one brief coaching lesson from the master. Worrell watched him bat. But by that time the great man had become a legend in his own lifetime. Richards and his friends played with homemade bats on which were scrawled the names 'Worrell' and 'Sobers'. Viv and his friends were playing cricket on the day Frank Worrell died. Everything stopped. Many of the players broke down in tears.

16

Antigua and the Windward and Leeward Islands making history. Under Richards' leadership they won the Shell Shield for the first time

'Obviously we were too young to know the great man,' says Richards, 'but from hearing others speak of what he had done, and from what we knew ourselves, Sir Frank was a West Indian hero and everyone was proud of him. He had made so many great runs against England and he had led his country. It was terribly sad to hear that he had died.'

Viv Richards did not help the new West Indian age into being. But he is a benefactor of its new-found pride and he decided to shoulder the responsibility it confers on the new breed of players. Anyone who fails to understand this can never hope to begin to understand West Indian cricket or Viv Richards.

In his first-ever test series in England, senior players regularly lectured the team about the need to make sure that their showing in test matches did not disappoint the hundreds of thousands of West Indians living in Britain. It's a responsibility that Richards bears willingly and ably.

The best-selling author and former Member of Parliament, Jeffrey Archer, writing a tribute to Viv Richards on the occasion of his benefit year, tells a story which goes some way to explaining why the contemporary West Indian cricketer must see his role in a far wider context than that circumscribed by the game alone:

'My son William, aged nine, was reading an aricle in *The Times* about the Brixton riots, and when he finished I tentatively asked him how he felt about the National Front's view that black people were somehow inferior.

' "Pathetic," he replied, "none of them can have seen Viv Richards at the crease." '

It's a story which comes close to explaining how Viv Richards sees himself and his cricket, and it's a story that Richards himself delights in telling. 'Yeah, man,' he says, 'it was very good of Jeffrey Archer to recount that story in my testimonial brochure.

His Somerset team-mate Peter Roebuck relates how he and Richards spent an entire evening having quite a heated argument about the political merits of the 'black power' movement. The thoughtful Roebuck found it impossible to shake his team-mate from the assured conviction that it was the movement of the future. Such a conviction, expressed by a man who likes to portray himself as apolitical, is evidence of the deep scars early West Indian society, and the West Indies Cricket Board, left on players for several generations.

CHAPTER TWO

I tole him over an' over
agen: Watch de ball man, watch
de ball like it hook to you eye

when you first goes in an' you doan know de pitch
Uh doan mean to poke,
but you jes got to watch what you doin'

this isn't no time for playing
the fool nor making no sport; this is cricket

Edward Braithwaite

Cricket has always had a greater dimension in West Indian life than in England, Australia, India, Pakistan or New Zealand.

The West Indian writer and philosopher, C.L.R. James illustrates the point with memorable clarity. In his book *Beyond a Boundary* he tells the story of a village cricketer, Matthew Bondman. 'He was', says James, 'an awful character. He was generally dirty. He would not work. His eyes were fierce, his language was violent and his voice was loud. His lips curled back naturally and he intensified it by an almost perpetual snarl. My grandmother and aunts detested him. He would often without shame walk up the main street barefooted, "with his planks on the ground" as my grandmother would report. He did it often and my grandmother must have seen it hundreds of times, but she never failed to report it. ... The whole Bondman family, except for the father, was unsatisfactory. It was from his mother that Matthew had inherited or absorbed his flair for language and invective. His sister, Marie, was quiet but bad, and despite all circumlocutions, or perhaps because of them, which my aunts employed, I knew it had something to do with men. But the two families were linked. They rented from us, they had lived there for a long time, and their irregularity of life exercised its fascination for my puritanical aunts. But that is not why I remember Matthew. For ne'er-do-well, in fact vicious, character, as he was, Matthew had one saving grace – Matthew could bat. More than that, Matthew, so crude and

19

vulgar in every aspect of his life, with a bat in his hand was all grace and style. When he practised on an afternoon with the local club, people stayed to watch and walked away when he was finished ... My aunts were uncompromising in their judgments of him and yet,' says James, 'my grandmother's oft-repeated verdict: "Good for nothing except to play cricket" did not seem right to me. How could an ability to play cricket atone in any sense for Matthew's abominable way of life?'

So writing about his childhood in the West Indies at the turn of the century, C.L.R. James was, by the example of his puritanical aunts, made aware of a crucial fact. There was something about an ability to play cricket which seemed to set one apart, even to atone for one's failings. Bondman was a villain. But even the old ladies of the village, who so detested his character, were forced to add the rider that Matthew Bondman could bat.

As a young man, James acquired a passion for Greek and English literature and for cricket. And he came to the following conclusion: 'Cricket is a game of high and difficult technique. If it were not, it could not carry the load of social response and implications which it carries.' That the game survived and flourished in West Indian islands, where every facet of community life was torn apart by stark social divisions, is a tribute to its residual strength. As far as the literature of cricket was concerned, James writes of having read this description of a famous eighteenth century cricketer:

> Beldham was great in every hit, but his peculiar glory was the cut. Here he stood, with no man beside him, the laurel was all his own; it seemed like the cut of a racket. His wrists seemed to turn on springs of the finest steel. He took the ball as Burke did the House of Commons, between wind and water – not a moment too soon or late.

The divisions in society were accurately mirrored in the composition of the cricket clubs in Trinidad. A decision about joining one of the established clubs at the turn of the century – and indeed right up until the early 1970s – was not a simple one.

The best clubs for first-class cricket were organised on straight colour lines. By far the best in Trinidad was, and perhaps still is, the Queen's Park Cricket Club. The club owned the Queen's Park Oval, where all the inter-island fixtures and all the test matches are played. The membership of the Queen's Park Club was white. It was easier for a camel to go through the eye of a needle than for a black man to become a member of the Queen's Park Club.

Because the club had the best facilities, and because of its prestige in the running of the game at international level, its white members had a considerable advantage over those players who could not belong. For more than fifty years, there was hardly one solitary voice of dissent to be heard about this state of affairs, in a country where the vast majority of the people was black.

Today, it is incredible to recall that shortly after Trinidad achieved independence from Britain in 1962, the Government of the day was forced, by an incident at a tennis and social club, to set up a Commission of Inquiry to look into the practice of racial discrimination in Trinidad life.

The Hilton Hotel in Port of Spain had arrived at an arrangement with the nearby Trinidad Country Club which enabled hotel guests to play tennis there. (There were, at the time, no tennis courts at the Hilton.) On the day of the incident in question, the Trinidad Country Club was informed that two American guests wanted to play.

The arrival of two black Americans threw the club officials into a state of considerable confusion. In an embarrassing and muddled explanation, they explained either that the arrangement with the Hilton had been terminated or that there were no free tennis courts available. Shocked and alarmed at this, the Americans returned to the hotel to complain to the Manager of Public Relations. Just as they were describing to her what had happened, another guest walked in to thank her for having arranged his enjoyable game at the Country Club. Needless to say, the guest who did manage to play was white.

What is particularly significant about that incident is the fact that the club might well have chosen to let the two black Americans play, recognising that it had been caught by a blanket arrangement with the Trinidad Hilton, and try in some clever way to make sure no other blacks got through. But even two were too many. There was to be no breach of the colour line.

C.L.R. James summed up the question of clubs and the complexities caused by various shades of colour in this way:

The Negroid population of the West Indies is composed of a large percentage of actually black people and about fifteen or twenty per cent of people who are a varying combination of white and black. From the days of slavery, these have always

21

claimed superiority to the ordinary black, and a substantial majority of them still do so (though resenting as bitterly black assumptions of white superiority). With emancipation in 1834, the blacks themselves established a middle class. But between the brown-skinned middle class and the black, there is a continual rivalry, distrust and ill-feeling, which, skilfully played upon by the European peoples, poisons the life of the community. Where so many crosses and colours meet and mingle the shades are naturally difficult to determine and the resulting confusion is immense. There are the nearly white hanging on tooth and nail to the fringes of white society, and these, as it is easy to understand, hate contact with the darker skin far more than some of the broad-minded whites. Then there are the browns, intermediates, who cannot by any stretch of the imagination pass as white, but who will not go one inch towards mixing with people darker than themselves ... Associations are formed of brown people who will not admit into their number those too much darker than themselves and will have heated arguments in committee as to whether such and such a person's skin is fair enough to allow him or her to be admitted without lowering the tone of the institution. Clubs have been known to accept the daughter who was fair and refused the father who was black ... Fair-skinned girls who marry dark men are often ostracized by their families and given up for lost.

This was the kind of 'club' mentality which has always had a say in the selection of West Indian cricket teams. It was never quite possible to ignore abundant talent in players whatever their colour. (Although some selections were certainly curious to say the least. But not only in the West Indies is this the case.) But before Frank Worrell, the captain of the West Indies cricket team was always, and almost statutorily, white. And the West Indies Cricket Board of Control went to the most extraordinary lengths to make sure this unwritten 'rule', which no one would ever admit existed, was never broken.

It followed quite naturally, therefore, that a place always had to be found in every team selection for the statutory white player, and frequently more than one, in case of injuries.

Some of the white West Indian captains who led teams to England in the 1920s and 1930s had never even met the players. No one in the islands made a sound of protest. The West Indian islands were colonies: they were governed from London and there was no indigenous 'political' voice of dissent.

It is amazing to reflect now that neither the great George Headley nor Learie Constantine ever led the West Indies. The manoeuvrings of the West Indian Cricket Board from the 1950s to make sure no black man ever did, were to be quite exceptional.

In the words of *Wisden*, the 1950 West Indies team to England 'reached maturity on their seventh visit to the cradle of cricket'. The West Indies won three out of four tests, and the two architects of their success, Sonny Rhamadhin and Alfred Valentine, had calypsos sung about them in their honour. The two spinners shared 258 wickets on the tour.

But two other West Indian players also excelled on that tour, in a manner which marked them out for great things in the future. When *Wisden* came to choose the five young cricketers of 1950, there were four West Indian players: Rhamadhin, Valentine, Frank Worrell and Everton Weekes. *Wisden* again: 'The three coloured players from the tiny island of Barbados, Weekes, Worrell and Walcott, stood out in a class of their own.' (Intending no criticism whatever, it's interesting to note the ease with which *Wisden* had slipped into what had been in effect the language of West Indies cricket, in talking about 'coloured players'.)

Worrell's 261 in the third test against England at Trent Bridge, where he and Everton Weekes put on 283 runs for the third wicket, was described as 'a masterpiece'. 'For beauty of stroke,' the *Cricketers Almanack* wrote, 'no one in the history of the game can have excelled Worrell. Lean, a fairly tall figure, there was something like a dreamy casualness about the way he flicked the ball to the boundary.'

What *Wisden* saw in 1950, many West Indians had known for some time. But the West Indies Board of Control continued to see players like Worrell as team members, never in the responsible role of team leadership. To accuse the West Indian cricket authorities of those days of racism might perhaps be wide of the mark. More accurate would be the observation that they were simply captives of a pernicious social myopia. It had just never occurred to them that a team representing the West Indies in England, Australia or New Zealand should be led by anyone who was not in their view 'socially acceptable'. To be socially acceptable in the West Indies society of that day, one had to be white.

The conquering West Indies team of 1950 returned to the islands as heroes. The captain had been John Goddard, a white Barbadian. But Goddard, a prolific left-handed batsman who had once shared in a stand of 502 runs with Frank Worrell in representative Island competition, could not be faulted. He had done his job well and had earned the distinction of leading the West Indies to their first-ever victory in a series over England.

The story from 1950 onwards, though, takes a fascinating turn. When the West Indies went back to England seven years later, May and Cowdrey had developed a technique for dealing with the spin of Rhamadhin and Valentine. Cowdrey used his pads much more than his bat and the West Indies were comprehensively beaten. About the only distinction for the West Indies on that tour was Worrell's carrying his bat for 191 in the Trent Bridge test.

The 1950s were marked by a change in the political climate in the West Indies. Senior West Indian politicians had some years before begun to advance the case for the islands to have a greater say in the way they were governed. Success on the cricket field in 1950 had helped. At Trent Bridge and Headingley the colonised had proved themselves to be the equal of the colonisers.

There were political opponents of this move towards independence, but perhaps one of the few institutions to completely ignore the spirit of the times was the West Indian Cricket Board.

To cement their political grip on the islands against the almost certain growth of nationalist pressures, the expatriate rulers of the islands had formed an alliance with the local whites. In exchange, the local whites sought, and were granted, privilege – perhaps the richest reward of all in the colonies. They got the top jobs, their views carried the most weight in society and they belonged to the best clubs ... even cricket clubs. White privilege also meant the automatic exclusion of the underprivileged – blacks. By their machinations throughout the 1950s, the West Indies cricket bosses placed themselves firmly in the camp of those who represented that privilege, and who were, by definition, hostile to any rising nationalism. And the West Indies Cricket Board did this by maintaining an unstated but firm policy that the captain of the West Indies cricket team should be white.

The lengths to which they went to ensure that their policy was never traversed showed a determination so firm that it effectively rules out any theories to the contrary. One view is that while all this went on, the people of the islands remained largely passive and uncomplaining. The other is that, by their actions, the West Indies cricket authorities had set a time-bomb ticking away loudly under a corrupt edifice of their own creation.

When, in 1960, a crowd invaded the Queen's Park Oval and threw bottles, it was not so much because they were annoyed that one of the local batsmen had been given out in a test match which the West Indies were losing badly anyway, but because the crowd felt that the old alliance was at work again, openly siding with the visiting MCC team. So well had the alliance worked over the years that at any test match against England in the West Indies there was always the surprising fact of a sizeable proportion of the spectators who identified with, and rooted for, the visitors. The spectacle of this – and its implied contempt for any nationalist sensibilities – had always rankled in the mind of the black West Indian. The crowd's action that day in 1960 was a protest against forces seen to be operating against the best interests of West Indies cricket.

Having led the West Indies to victory in England in 1950, it was not surprising that Goddard should lead the team to Australia and New Zealand the following year.

On 9 November in Brisbane, the West Indies were up against an Australian team which included the then formidable and now legendary names, Morris, Hassett, Harvey, Miller, Lindwall, Ring, Johnson and Langley, and later in the tour Benaud, who made his debut against the tourists in Sydney. The West Indies were easily beaten, one of the few highlights of their tour being a superb display of controlled medium-paced bowling by Worrell in Adelaide when he sent back six Australian batsmen for a mere 38 runs.

In New Zealand the West Indies won the first test comfortably, and the second drawn game was marked by the batting of the three Ws: Weekes got 51, Worrell 100 and Walcott 115.

J.B. Stollmeyer, who had made his debut in 1939 at the age of eighteen against England at Lords, was chosen as captain of the West Indies side to play the visiting Indians in 1952/53. Four of the five test matches ended in stalemate, the West Indies taking the rubber by the only game which was concluded, the third test in Barbados, which they won by 142 runs. For India, Polly Umrigar got a fine century in the first Port of Spain test, but the rest of the series was dominated by the power of the West Indies batting. In the first test Everton Weekes scored a double century, and when the teams returned to Trinidad for the third test encounter, he got 161. At

Bourda, in what was then British Guiana, Worrell made 56, Weekes 86 and Walcott 125. In the fifth test in Jamaica, the three Ws took all the batting honours: Worrell made a magnificent 237, Weekes got 109 and Walcott weighed in with 118.

The West Indies had beaten India under the captaincy of the competent Jeffrey Stollmeyer, but the contributions of the three Ws to the team's overall performance had been so substantial that it seemed only a matter of time before one of these outstanding players should lead the West Indies team.

But with the visit of the England team to the West Indies in 1953/54, it was not to be. So firmly entrenched had the policy of the West Indies Board become, that it is probably true to say that not even the most radical thinker of the day was bold enough to predict that the breakthrough of a black West Indies captain would come in a series against England or Australia. The common saying about 'horses for courses' had developed a new connotation in the West Indian mind: surely for a visiting team from England, there must be a white West Indies captain? And so it was. Jeffrey Stollmeyer was again asked to lead the West Indies.

From a West Indian point of view, it was a disappointing series. Having beaten England convincingly in the first two tests in Kingston and Bridgetown, England won the third in Georgetown by nine wickets. The fourth in Port of Spain was fought to a high-scoring draw, but England returned to Sabina Park in Jamaica to win the fifth test and to square the series, two tests all. The England victory in Jamaica in the fifth test in April 1954 was distinguished by a remarkable spell of bowling by Trevor Bailey, who absolutely demolished the West Indies batting by taking seven wickets for 34 runs.

But again, aside from the fact that Conrad Hunte got an unavailing double century in the final test match and that a young player named Garfield Sobers made his debut in that same test, the batting of the three Ws was the scourge of the England bowlers. In Barbados Walcott scored a double century and effectively set up the West Indies victory. In the drawn fourth test in Trinidad the three Ws tore the English attack to shreds. This time the double century was scored by Weekes. Cutting and driving superbly, he scored 206. Frank Worrell was all ease and grace in his 167 and 'big' Clyde Walcott, who hit the ball harder than anyone could remember, ham-

OPPOSITE The great Frank Worrell in action (*Press Association*)

mered his way to 124. It was a feast of runs (the West Indies made 681 in one innings) and glorious strokeplay against the Englishmen, on the ground that Trinidadians like to believe is the home of West Indian cricket. Few West Indian crowds have been witness before or since to anything like the 338 partnership between Weekes and Worrell.

And there was the prospect of even more test cricket. Less than a year after the England team left, the Australians were due to arrive in the West Indies for a five-test series.

On the eve of their arrival, the West Indies Board surpassed itself. In pursuit of its policy of choosing an 'acceptable' West Indies captain, its scheming became positively Machiavellian. The Board had also obviously decided that its position was so unassailable, it had become so much a part of the ruling alliance, that it could afford to treat the views of the people of the West Indies with contempt. It remains one of the darker, less-inspiring chapters in the history of West Indies cricket.

Not many years later, Clyde Walcott, in his book *Island Cricketers* described the extraordinary manoeuvrings of the Board thus:

> Before the Australians arrived, the West Indies Board did something which at first seemed strange in announcing the names of the captain and vice-captain for our tour of New Zealand which was to take place almost a year later. The names were Denis Atkinson and Bruce Pairaudeau. Only after this announcement had sunk in – and caused a great deal of controversy – did the Board announce that Jeff Stollmeyer and Denis Atkinson would be captain and vice-captain respectively for the Australian series about to start.

The monumental travesty of what the Board did must be placed in some sort of context. Frank Worrell had been vice-captain in the series against the MCC only a few months before. Yet even that was to be denied him now. Needless to say, the newcomers to high office, Atkinson and Pairaudeau, like Stollmeyer, were white.

After that, what seemed a convoluted plot becomes terribly simple. Because New Zealand was not considered a front-ranking test-match-playing country, the West Indies had decided, well in advance it seems, not to send the best available team there. So the inexperienced Atkinson and the even less experienced Pairaudeau were chosen to take the touring side to New Zealand. Having made that decision, for reasons which could never be justified in logic, the next step was to find some way of giving Atkinson some much needed 'experience'. The only way to do that was to make him Stollmeyer's deputy in the series against Australia. But the gods have a way of punishing this kind of blatant unreason; and so they did.

Just before the first test against Australia, Stollmeyer was injured and pronounced himself unavailable for the first test. So Denis Atkinson, who was not even the regular captain of his island side, had been dug up from obscurity and catapulted into the leadership of the star-studded West Indies team. It was almost barbaric.

The Australians crushed the West Indies. Atkinson did not lead the team for the entire series, but the slide began under him in the Kingston test. Australia's victory there was set up by centuries from Harvey and Miller. Walcott and Worrell dutifully supported their new captain with hundreds in reply, but Australia walked away with the game by nine wickets.

Stollmeyer led the West Indies in the second and third tests, by the end of which Australia had gone two up in the series. Atkinson was captain in the drawn fourth test, in which he put on 348 runs for the seventh wicket with DePeiza. And the West Indies were again under Atkinson's captaincy when Harvey, Miller, Archer and Benaud made hundreds (Benaud's coming in 78 minutes) and when Australia put the issue beyond all doubt.

Clyde Walcott wrote his name into the record books in that series. In the second and fifth tests he scored a century in each innings, becoming the only player to do that twice in the same rubber.

Towards the end of 1955 Denis Atkinson duly took the team to New Zealand. In each of the three test matches, Everton Weekes took a century off the home team and the West Indies ran away with all three tests.

But to the mainstays of the West Indian side, the indignity they were being made to suffer was far from over. John Goddard was recalled to take the West Indies to England in 1957, although Walcott was made vice-captain. *Wisden* relates that when neither Goddard nor Walcott was available, 'Worrell showed unmistakable gifts of leadership.' But there was, alas, a long way to go before he would be called upon to demonstrate those gifts.

This time May and Cowdrey mastered the West Indies' spin attack, which had mesmerised the England batsmen in 1950, and Goddard's 1957 team were roundly defeated.

But all was not gloom for the West Indies Board. A Cambridge Blue, Gerry Alexander, had made his debut on 25 July in the Headingley test of that ill-fated tour. By January of the following year, with Weekes and Walcott in the party, Alexander was named West Indies captain. He lacked experience – but he was white. In any other sport and in another time, there would long ago have been a fullscale revolution at this appalling state of affairs. But in the West Indies there was only smouldering resentment among the population, and corrosive discontent among senior players. Alexander led the West Indies against Pakistan and India and was captain again in the 1959/60 series against England (when bottles were thrown at the Queen's Park Oval in Port of Spain).

The people had had enough. The obscenity of appointing Alexander as captain of a team of which Frank Worrell was a member became a major talking-point in the West Indies in 1960. The organ of a new nationalist party in Trinidad was a paper called *The Nation*, and its editor, C.L.R. James, almost singlehandedly waged a campaign for the replacement of Alexander by Worrell. For a long time, the bosses of West Indian cricket maintained an Olympian silence. But with the force of an idea which has reached its time, the 'Frank Worrell for Captain' bandwagon rolled on. It proved unstoppable and Worrell was asked to take the West Indies to Australia.

The captaincy of Frank Worrell, after such a well-publicised campaign, could not have been divorced from contemporary political developments. The heavily British-sponsored West Indies Federation of 1958 had broken up and Jamaica and Trinidad, soon to be followed by Barbados and Guyana, were moving to independence. So the change of attitude forced on the West Indies Board coincided with the march to political freedom and nationhood. With Worrell's captaincy, West Indies cricket had broken into a new age, an age in which Sobers, Kanhai, Lloyd, Hall, Richards and countless others were to feel quite differently about what they represented. The career of Viv Richards was to mirror that change.

CHAPTER THREE

No Vivi – No match

Antiguan crowd

Viv Richards was born in 1952 in Antigua, one of the smaller West Indian islands. Unlike Jamaica, Trinidad, Guyana and Barbados (the 'big four'), Antigua had never made a mark on West Indian cricket.

This is not to suggest that cricket was not played in Antigua. Indeed, Viv's father was a competent allrounder who represented the island for many years, and one of his brothers was also a good club player.

But the development of cricket and any progress towards broadening the representative nature of the West Indies team was slow. And for many years islands like Antigua, St Vincent and Montserrat could only look with envy at what the smaller territories came to regard as the 'big four', the four countries whose players made up the West Indies team. Cricket prominence seemed to follow economic development. And on this basis, there was no way that little Antigua, with a total area of one hundred square miles, could compete.

Trinidad, for example, had oil. The refining company Texaco ploughed money into providing adequate facilities for cricket in the south of the country, and their efforts were rewarded with the discovery of players like Sonny Rhamadhin. The sugar belt was in Central Trinidad. And in that part of the country Tate and Lyle, who ran the sugar plantations, poured money into the game. The capital, Port of Spain, was of course the home of the famous Queen's Park Cricket Club and the home of the equally famous Queen's Park Savannah. The Savannah had nothing of the sophistication of the Queen's Park Oval, nor were the playing surfaces anywhere near as good. But on a Saturday afternoon there could be as many as twenty cricket matches, at club level, dotted across the expanse of the Queen's Park Savannah.

Similarly, Jamaica, the largest West Indian island in the English-speaking cricket-playing group, gained a considerable reputation as an exporter of bauxite, sugar and bananas. Guyana also exported bauxite and rice in commercially viable quantities and Barbados was well-known as *the* tourist paradise in the Caribbean. It also had sugar.

Antigua could lay claim to none of these economic distinctions and for many years its economy, like its cricket, languished in the general backwardness of the smaller islands in the Caribbean chain. Certainly, Horatio Nelson had taken a great liking to Antigua's harbour, later to be known as Nelson's Dockyard, but not a great deal of prosperity went with the totally justified reputation that tiny Antigua possessed the finest naval base in the entire region.

Richards was born into a happy, lower middleclass West Indian family. In the West Indies of the early 1950s that meant that the family was not desperately poor, but that money was always scarce and stretching the meagre resources to provide for everyone required skill and ingenuity.

Vivian's father, Malcolm Richards, was a warder at the local prison. His cricket made him a popular extrovert. Vivian's mother, Gretel, is a quiet, sensitive, thoughtful lady, who, in the matriarchal tradition of West Indian family life, was responsible for her children's religious upbringing and their secular education.

West Indian parents of the period were obsessed with the education of their children. The colonial tradition had glorified Oxford and Cambridge as internationally known centres of academic excellence and every West Indian parent wanted one of two things for his offspring: he or she must either be a doctor or a lawyer. It was the only certain way of ensuring that one's children would do better in life than their parents had done, the only certain way that the succeeding generation would move out of the 'class' into which they were born.

After the second world war, there was another recognised route to greater social mobility: becoming a famous cricketer. Medicine, law and cricket – those were then the avenues open to young West Indians to climb the social scale, not an unimportant consideration in colonies where the English class system had arrived with the colonisers.

So his mother ensured that young Vivian regularly attended and participated in services in the Anglican church in the capital, St John's. And he was sent to a small private school.

Richards Senior (second from right, back row) in the victorious Windward Leeward team in 1946, winners of the Hesketh Bell Shield

Such was the parental determination that children should be driven to academic success that something approaching a private tutor was invariably found to supplement whatever teaching was provided by the state system. The need for what had come to be known as 'a decent education' was paramount in the minds of all West Indian parents.

Young Vivian Richards showed no signs of academic brilliance, but he did well enough to win a scholarship to Antigua Grammar School. He performed creditably in a few subjects, but his popularity derived more from his easy charm and his sporting athleticism.

It was at Antigua Grammar that young Richards showed promise with the cricket bat. For a time, he seemed anxious to win a place in his school eleven by bowling slow off-breaks. This was certainly a departure from the most common West Indian passion, which is the desire to bowl fast. West Indian schoolboys of the period took for themselves the names of famous fast bowlers and tried to copy what

33

LEFT Richards' parents outside their home in Antigua, 1983

ABOVE Brother Mervyn with his family and Miriam in Antigua

they felt was the style of those players. There was always a respectable sprinkling of Wes Halls and Ray Lindwalls in dusty West Indian backyards.

He was soon representing his school, batting well down the order and turning his off-breaks a mile on rough uneven pitches. He decided to devote more time to his batting when he was called for 'chucking'.

Away from school, Richards played most of his cricket in 'matches' and 'competitions' hastily arranged and on 'pitches' which were under inches of wild grass and other thick vegetation only hours before the first ball was bowled.

With no real facilities, except for the occasional good school wicket, young West Indians had to show initiative. On the morning of a big match – which would usually mean a team from one side of a tiny street playing against a team from the other – five or six players would be deputed to clear the wild ground for the wicket.

There was never any attempt to secure the prior consent of the owner of the piece of land in question for its use as a big-match venue. But few landowners were ever displeased at having part of their holding cleared. Sometimes, the teams got lucky and it was common land. Occasionally, there were problems of getting rid of the cows and goats, grazing around first slip or extra cover, but these were considered minor irritations. Far more serious was the fact that after a hard morning's toil clearing the ground, in searing temperatures, and trying to get a stretch of 22 yards roughly in shape, the result was still far from acceptable. There would be cow pats all over the bowler's run-up, large holes in the middle of the uneven surface, deep cracks scarring the entire wicket, odd tree stumps which proved immovable and awkward ridges just where the good-length delivery could be expected to land.

Richards confirms today that such surfaces never once prevented a match from starting on time. Surveying the wicket and the surrounding bush (because clearing a space for a wicket was as much as could be done in one morning) the usual decision of the committee of small boys was invariably: 'Come, leh we still play.'

At times, there were attempts to 'roll' the pitch. An old drum, filled with stones for weight, was the roller and buckets of water liberally fed into the most difficult parts of the wicket accounted for that side of the wicket preparation. Sometimes, there'd be the assistance of a proper groundsman, but it could never be counted on.

Very rarely, there would be proper cricket bats. Some lucky boys did have them, but they were prized possessions, generally given by parents, not as birthday gifts but as rewards for doing well in end-of-term exams at school. Few teams of eight or nine boys had as many as three bats, and since some youngsters were understandably reluctant to have too many others use their bats, homemade blades were popular, as were batting pads, crudely fashioned from strips of cardboard. There was hardly ever more than one pair of proper pads, and wicket-keeping gloves and batting gloves were a rare sight. So each batsman wore a single pad, and the keeper, if he were lucky, would have availed himself of a pair of workman's gloves. But much more common was the sight on a sunny Saturday afternoon of a wicket keeper standing up to a fast bowler with neither the comfort nor the security of wicket-keeping pads or gloves.

Batting in cricket at this level could be a hazardous business. The most important asset was quickness of eye to cope with the unpredictability of the pitch and the delivery which suddenly reared off

the ground. Survival at the crease for any length of time depended on the batsman's ability to adjust quickly to varying bounce and to deliveries which were just plain erratic.

Some strokes were also ruled out in the circumstances, and others could be played with impunity and to the batsman's advantage. There was, for example, never a great deal of profit to be derived from playing too defensively. The uneven surface of many pitches made it impossible to predict when a good-length ball might defeat even the most carefully placed defensive bat. And when a ball was there to be hit, even when hitting it meant playing across the line, then it was perhaps advisable to do so. The most profitable stroke in such rudimentary conditions was the hook shot. Anything short of a length could be despatched behind square with impunity. There were hardly ever any fielders in the overgrown outfield, whereas plodding or pushing tentatively forward could result in being snapped up at one of the catching positions close to the wicket. There was always a great deal of merit in hitting the cover off the ball.

Those deliveries which did not lend themselves to being hooked were played off the back foot. To this day, West Indian players are some of the most accomplished back-foot players in the game. On bad pitches the ball which deviated unexpectedly off the wicket was to be cut, or driven through cover. In the tropics most quick bowlers got more movement off the seam than in the air.

Richards also learnt from his earliest experiences that slow bowlers could not be played with any skill if a batsman's feet were firmly anchored at the crease. A spinning ball on a bad wicket was liable to do anything. The delivery had to be met, and the spin killed before the ball had the time to do everything the bowler intended it to do. That is how using one's feet to the spin bowler became a West Indian hallmark. With a minimum of movement through the air, there were few medium-paced bowlers. Those who tried were hit out of the park. Bowlers were either very fast, or clever spinners of the ball. To this day the characteristics of West Indian batting reflect the way batsmen were compelled to play by the wickets on which they learnt their craft.

The other popular venue for cricket in the West Indies was the

OPPOSITE Richards' most important asset is his quickness of eye – be it hitting the ball out of the ground . . .

(INSET) . . . or, with more finesse, sweeping to leg (both ASP)

beach. Antigua, where Viv Richards was born, has scores of beautiful stretches of white sand. Young West Indians aren't very good at lying quietly on beaches: they either swim or play cricket. In its popularity, beach cricket spawned rules of its own. Horizontal lines, marking out a space the width of about nine cricket stumps, were drawn in the sand. The batsman had to guard that space. Anything which he failed to touch on its way through that space was out. Bowlers got wickets by speed (not easy on the docile sand so 'throwing', or 'chucking', was not uncommon) or by guile. Since there could be as many as twenty fielders near the bat, the most effective shot was the straight drive, hit hard and all along the ground. The other sure winner was the hook shot, over the heads of the in fielders and into the surf.

This was the nature of the 'school' in which Viv Richards learnt the game.

The other great beach game was, of course, football. And even when it was clear that he had an exceptionally good eye for stroking the cricket ball, Richards was still uncertain whether he should devote more time to soccer than to cricket.

Counselled repeatedly by his school master to 'hit the ball straight' and not 'across the line', and by his father to stay at the crease long enough to acquire a 'big score', Vivian, not yet in his teens, became captain of his grammar school team. By this time, books were beginning to take a poor second place to his cricket. Having never batted higher than five or six, Vivian used the captain's prerogative to promote himself to what has remained his favourite position, number three.

Perhaps success of this kind came much too early. The young Richards, who loved to defy all the coaching manuals, to play across the line and bang the ball through mid-wicket, had developed sharp reflexes and an arrogant feeling of invincibility. He regarded all bowlers with lofty disdain. Although he has acquired greater technique along the way, and although he has become more patient and responsible over the years, he has only ever been troubled by one bowler.

He scored four centuries for his grammar school, but his batting lacked consistency. He was frequently out, caught in the deep, hooking intemperately before he'd had a chance to have a good look at the bowling. The captain found himself left out on several occasions.

Off the field, young Richards was still the quiet charming school-boy whose distinctive voice made him such an accomplished singer in the church choir, much to his mother's delight. With a bat in his hand, everything changed. He walked to the wicket with a confident swagger and played every ball with a graceful contempt.

Neither his schoolmaster's advice about not playing 'across the line' and holing out at mid-wicket, nor his father's injunction to have a good look at the bowling before launching an attack, made any impression on the mind of the young Antiguan. By the time he was fourteen, he had already scored several hundreds, but he was destined to pay a heavy price for his precocity.

Leaving school at eighteen, he joined a cricket club of which his brother was a member. But some time before that, he'd met a young cricketer by the name of Andy Roberts, and because Andy was a member of another club in St John's, Richards left his brother's club and was enrolled as a member of a club called Rising Sun.

These were wonderful days for young Richards. He was obviously a player of considerable talent, and very soon word of his batting prowess spread to every corner of little Antigua. 'Malcolm's boy, Vivian' was a name on the lips of all Antiguans who followed the game. As he was to do later in another town thousands of miles across the Atlantic, he singlehandedly doubled the number of people who watched Rising Sun, and his batting gave the club prestige and success it had never before enjoyed.

Even from those earliest days, Richards was totally committed to all departments of the game. When he was not making runs or teasing batsmen with his deliberate off-spin, he enjoyed the exhilaration of fielding at slip or in the gully. He's always been remarkably quick in the outfield – and many Antiguan club cricketers have painful memories of being run out by a Richards underarm throw at the stumps from cover.

Like all West Indians, he followed the exploits of the three Ws on distant cricket grounds in far-off lands. When the West Indies played in England, for the most part, work in the islands stopped until stumps were drawn for the day. Those who did report for work did so with transistors glued to their ears. When the West Indies played in Australia, India or Pakistan, hundreds of thousands of people turned up for work bleary eyed, having listened to radio commentaries of the test matches until three or four in the morning. Viv Richards did all this, while piling up the runs for his club.

Because his father had represented Antigua, the spotlight fell on him from the moment he first swung a bat. Now his abundant talent made it a foregone conclusion that he would play for his country.

All this still fell far short of what his parents had intended for young Vivian. His father had family connections in the United States and, although Vivian had not distinguished himself in school examinations, it was still hoped that by diligence and hard work at night school, he could perhaps become an engineer. Vivian was fascinated by the prospect of migrating to New York, but it's doubtful whether he ever seriously entertained the proposition that he could spend his evenings swotting with sufficient determination to become an engineer.

Today, he is still acutely sensitive about the fact that he acquired no academic distinction; and his relations with people who have are perhaps at the heart of a taut and complex personality. He secretly admires in others the success they've attained in an area where he failed. But his admiration has well-defined limits. Although he is unfailingly friendly, he keeps his intellectual superiors at arm's length.

He's had little time for books since his passion for cricket blossomed into the time-consuming business of full-time professionalism. And he reserves his most explosive bursts of temper for those occasions when, in conversation about world affairs or political concepts, he feels he's being challenged or, worse still, put on the defensive. The exchange would become especially heated if his interlocutor attempted to assert the primacy of an idea gained from a book.

Back in Antigua, he was drawn inexorably towards cricket in almost everything he did. His first job, in Darcy's Bar and Restaurant in St John's, came not because he displayed some hidden talent as a barman, but because the proprietor saw his potential as a cricketer and felt that he might be able to help the young player by keeping a closer eye on him if he worked in the restaurant. It was therefore no accident that the proprietor of Darcy's Bar and Restaurant gave Vivian Richards his first cricket bat. The job paid a handsome ten pounds a week with tips – good money in those days – and for a while Vivian was very proud to be able to help supplement the family income, especially when his father was not in regular work. But the job in Darcy's Restaurant didn't last long.

After less than a year, Vivian, a restless spirit, yearning to be successful in some enterprise, was persuaded that he might become

OPPOSITE At Darcy's in Antigua Viv was a poor barman

41

a good motor mechanic. In any event, a cousin told him, repairing cars and old tractors was not a bad approach to the ultimate goal of becoming an engineer. But after only a few months, Vivian decided that being an apprentice mechanic took him too far out of town to report on time for his weekend cricket matches. It was one thing to be late for work, but batting at number three, one could never be late for a match. Thus ended Vivian Richards' attempt to make his fame and fortune as a motor mechanic in Antigua.

By his nineteenth birthday, Vivian Richards was being talked about as the best prospect Antigua had ever had. Old men, who had never had even the limited opportunities which seemed to be opening up for a young batsman of promise, muttered sagely with eyes moistened by the pleasure of watching him drive elegantly through the covers, that 'Malcolm's boy' would one day play for the Leeward Islands, and perhaps go on to represent the West Indies.

Confident though he was of his own ability, Richards never let his thoughts drift that far into the future. He had seen the great Gary Sobers bat in the Leeward Islands and on one occasion, perhaps the most memorable trip of his young years, he'd been taken to Bridgetown to see the West Indies in a test match. Sobers, his hero, had taken a fine century off the New Zealanders and Vivian thought he would never see anything better in his whole life. Even his youthful confidence fell short of allowing him to think that he could one day emulate the great man.

The possibility seemed even more remote when he was involved in an altercation with the cricket authorities in the Leeward Islands which scarred his psyche for life.

Thanks mainly to Richards' style and explosive batting, Antiguan cricket had rapidly become the jewel in the crown of Leeward Islands cricket. Viv Richards was the man the spectators came to watch. One day Antigua were playing the sister island of St Kitts. Cricket is not only played in the West Indies, it is talked about incessantly and expansively. And on that day, sixteen-year-old Viv Richards was also doing a fair amount of the talking.

It was the first game of the 1968/69 season. Richards had been in exceptional form, and had not been afraid to speculate what terrors lay in store for the hapless bowlers from neighbouring St Kitts from the broad bat of Viv Richards.

The first wicket fell cheaply, but no one minded. After all, the man walking out to bat at number three had frequently changed the fortunes of his side at a stroke. Within the space of a few balls, and before he had scored, Richards was adjudged caught at short leg. The phenomenon of seeing their hero fall for a 'duck' was met with silent incomprehension and abject consternation.

At the crease the cocky young batsman's own consternation took a far more demonstrative form. He glared at the umpire and truculently stood his ground, refusing to begin the long walk back to the pavilion. Not content with an open show of defiance, he walked down the track to remonstrate with the umpire. Only after several minutes did he eventually leave the wicket.

By that time the crowd, at first struck dumb by their hero's demise, was silent no longer. Seeing in his protestations that a great injustice had been done, they took matters into their own hands: they invaded the ground to confront the 'erring' umpire and decided to sit on the wicket. Someone produced a placard with the words: 'No Viv – No Match.'

Richards today recalls the story with considerable embarrassment, and he is so mortified that he could have been involved in such a disgraceful incident that it is not always easy to accurately piece together precisely how the incident developed from that point.

His behaviour and the invasion of the ground put the authorities in an impossible position. They could have stood their ground, and acted in full support of the umpire by abandoning the match, if the crowd insisted on occupying the field of play. Instead, they took the extraordinary decision to invite Richards to return to the crease. It had been a full two hours since he was given out.

Even to this day Richards still feels that he had been 'set up' by the cricket administrators, whose only concern at the time had been to make sure that their game of cricket was not stopped by the crowd's displeasure. He feels very much that he was the pawn in a much larger game, although he always admits that the whole incident was caused by the fact that he behaved badly. He says:

When I think back about that now, that's the first thing I must say: it was all started by me. It was my fault. I behaved very badly and I am not proud of it. But the second thing is that those in authority, who were advising me, didn't do themselves very proud either. You see, I was told that to restore the peace I should go back out to bat. I did not want to, and I was not very happy about it. But I went. I was young and I suppose I was

43

inexperienced and easily led, you know. So I went back to bat, you could say against my own better judgment.

And then, having done what they had asked, when I came back in and after the match and all that, they held this meeting and decided to ban me for two years. I felt I deserved some punishment, but I also felt it was a bit harsh when you think I was banned by the same people who had asked me to go back to bat. And they didn't even have the courtesy to tell me to my face. I heard the news on the radio.

I could have taken the ban and forgotten it in time, had it not been for the fact that it became front-page news and was discussed in newspaper editorials. And people started to make nasty remarks to my parents and friends about my lack of sportsmanship. They would pass by my father's house and shout hurtful things. I couldn't even go to the movies. It was really an awful time for me. But that's the West Indian crowd for you. At least I learnt that. One day, you're a king and they can't do enough for you. The next day, you're out of favour and they'll throw stones at you. It's tough, but that's the way they play the game.

In the end, I think it all worked out in my favour. It gave me the inspiration to do what I think is right and not be led astray by others for their own ends. And it made me work harder to do well to prove those people wrong. I wanted to prove I was a good player and a good sportsman, despite what had happened. Sometimes in your career you need incidents like this to drive you to realise your full potential. You need the aggro, man, to push you on to greater things. I feel I am a better person because of what happened. I know what it is to be despised. And it was all the more sweeter when I got back into the crowd's good books. It's a really nice feeling to come back to the top from the bottom. That's really a great feeling. But I must confess, I never really forgot how they treated me when I was out of favour.

Batting a record second time in the same innings, Richards was again out without scoring. Extraordinarily, he also failed to score when Antigua batted a second time. The only flash of humour he allows himself about the incident now is his observation that perhaps

OPPOSITE No Vivi – No match!

44

no other player in the history of the game can claim to have made three noughts in the same match.

Richards learnt a great deal from that incident. It was the starting-point for his distrust of the West Indies cricket establishment: he felt he'd been badly advised by them, used, and then punished. And the memory of the manner in which the same fans who so adored his batting turned on him for his lack of sportsmanship remains with him to this day. He has never fully understood why the change in people's attitude to him had been so abrupt.

It's one of the reasons why he never lets himself get too close to people, even his staunchest supporters. He has become, since that incident, a very private man, to whom few but his most intimate friends ever get near. The incident had its salutary side: it curbed his youthful arrogance. He also learnt to keep his temper on a tight rein. Once it had got the better of him, and had let him down.

On his return to the game after his two-year suspension, he seems to have become a more mature player. He scored 127 and 87 for Antigua against St Kitts, and this was followed by two other hundreds in successive games and another sparkling century against Montserrat. By the time he approached his twenty-first birthday, his earlier indiscretion behind him, Viv Richards was about to represent the Leeward Islands in a regional tournament which had been started only a few years earlier, and which enabled cricketers from the smaller islands like Antigua to play against representative teams from Trinidad, Guyana, Jamaica and Barbados.

If a player proved himself in competition at this level, nothing stood in the way of his representing the West Indies. The Shell Shield Tournament, as it's called, brought together the best players in the Caribbean and was the proving ground for future West Indian stars.

Despite his prowess with the cricket bat, however, Richards' parents still harboured the hope that he would 'make something of himself' in one of the accepted professions; they hadn't given up on his becoming an engineer. New York was deemed to be the most suitable place and, for once, Richards found it difficult to marshall too many sound arguments against the wishes of his parents.

His only other contact with the world outside the West Indies had been a six-week visit to England to attend the Alf Gover coaching school in South London. And although at the end of that visit he was still prepared to follow his parents' advice and go to New York to be trained for a profession, the England visit broadened his horizons, as far as playing cricket was concerned.

Richards' own account of the visit is vividly told:

> I will never forget my first visit to England. It was winter and I never knew it could get so dark so early in the afternoon.
>
> Andy Roberts and I had been sent over by the Voluntary Coaching Council of Antigua. You see, I was playing a lot of cricket and making a lot of runs, but I had never been coached as such. Ours was raw talent, very raw. So the guys on the coaching council thought it might be a good idea to send us to England.
>
> My first problem, aside from the English climate, was that I found it difficult to adapt myself to the business of being coached. I had played my cricket quite naturally. No one really told me what to do. I suppose I played instinctively.
>
> I came to Alf Gover with a wide open stance. That had suited my quite well, you see, because in Antigua I was playing on hard wickets where I could hit 'through the line of the ball'. Alf tried first to make me change my grip. He wanted to try to teach me to play with the left elbow well cocked. But he had problems getting me to do that. I felt it was too defensive a stance and it didn't seem to give me enough time to hit out if I wanted to.
>
> I did try to listen to what Alf said, though, about playing with bat and pad close together. I think he made me realise - although I didn't let on at the time - the importance of being technically correct, whether you're playing a defensive shot or trying to cover-drive. That's the most important thing I learnt.

For Viv Richards and his compatriot Andy Roberts, life in England away from Alf Gover's school in Wandsworth also had its problems.

> It was even more difficult adapting to living in England, even for the six weeks we were there. The Voluntary Coaching Council in Antigua didn't have much money and we were put up in a guesthouse near Putney owned by a woman from New Zealand. We had a very cold room with one of those meters you had to fill up with tenpenny pieces if you wanted to heat up the room. And I had this belief, you know, that we would run out of tenpenny pieces and we would both freeze to death in the night.

I felt really miserable. We could never get accustomed to re-membering to always keep enough tenpenny pieces for the meter if you wanted keep warm.

Things got so rough that we had to leave that cold room in the guesthouse. We just couldn't stay there any longer. We were very lucky in a way. Andy had a sister in Hackney. When we told her about the guesthouse she took pity on us, and when we told her about the awful food she decided that we should stay with her. That changed everything. We were now with our own people, eating our own kind of Caribbean food. I had some cousins in North London and they took me out and taught me about English pubs. I had never been to a pub before and had never tasted warm beer. For some reason, I began to drink a lot of draught Guinness.

Richards' first visit to England had not been a coaching or gastro-nomic success. But the visit left its mark and New York and the thought of the profession his parents wanted him to pursue began to recede. He says: 'I felt it might be nice to come back and see England in the summer when it wasn't that cold. I felt England owed me a slightly better time.'

Back in Antigua, though, his parents continued to make plans for his study in America. Not long before he began preparing to leave sunny Antigua, a meeting with a Somerset Cricket Club official and a cricket fanatic changed his life.

A glorious chapter in English county cricket and in West Indian cricket was about to be written.

CHAPTER FOUR

Viv is the best player on the island

Antiguan taxi driver, 1974

Cricket stories, like good wine, mature with age and improve with the telling, and when the stories are about the discovery on a tiny Caribbean island of the best batsman in the world, then the embellishments tend to be even more lavish.

Richards himself remarks how, even today when so many details of his early life are so well-known, he still occasionally hears some fan saying to the other how 'Viv Richards gave up a place at a college in New York, and the chance of a fine academic career, to play cricket for Somerset'.

The New York idea had been forced on him by his parents. And he was going to have to pay his way, working during the day and studying at night school. It was perhaps destined never to occur.

Colin Atkinson, the President of Somerset Cricket Club, but in 1974 club chairman, insists that his version of how Richards came to the county is the most accurate.

The Somerset vice-chairman, Len Creed, is a cricket fanatic who took touring teams to the West Indies in the English winter. Visitations from unofficial touring parties from England were not unusual in the West Indies. For many years, Jim Swanton and Derek Robbins had organised tours of this kind, by getting together fifteen or so players who had no other engagements for that winter. The squads were usually multinational, there'd always be a couple of players from India or Pakistan, and two or three big names in international or county cricket would invariably be persuaded to make the tour. So it was, for example, with Len Creed's touring club side, Mendip Acorns: Sadiq Mohammed and Derek Underwood were members of that touring side to Antigua.

As Colin Atkinson tells it, Len Creed was always claiming that he had found yet another undiscovered player who was destined to change the face of international cricket. Atkinson is in reality far more blunt about Len Creed's talent spotting, although in a most

49

genial and friendly way. 'Len,' says Atkinson, 'saw a good cricketer once every ten days.'

On his visit to Antigua in 1974, Len Creed carried with him a note from Colin Cowdrey, the former England captain, who had remarked that on a previous visit to the island he'd seen a promising young player, 'a young chap by the name of Vivian Richards'.

So the Somerset vice-chairman's first task when he arrived was to find Vivian Richards. And in a small island like Antigua, where everybody knows everyone else, and where one is particularly well-known if one plays cricket well, finding him was not difficult.

Len Creed, in fact, met not only Richards, but also a young quick bowler, Andy Roberts, on the same day. Roberts was about to go to England to play for Hampshire, and Creed was astonished to learn that there was the possibility that Richards might take up a half-offer to play for Oldham in the Lancashire League in the north of England.

The Somerset club vice-chairman decided it was his duty to ensure that Richards went to Somerset and to no other English club side.

Although he had acquired the dubious distinction of discovering 'a good cricketer once every ten days' for Somerset, Len Creed was, in fact, shrewd enough not to trust his own judgment entirely. He talked to another Antiguan player, Danny Livingstone, who felt that young Richards could do well in English county cricket. And, of course, he'd had the recommendation of Colin Cowdrey.

That was just as well because the first time he saw Richards play the young batsman was not terribly impressive. He was well stumped before he had scored, but sensing how important the 'trial' was for Richards, the umpire, a compatriot, turned down the loud appeal.

Given a second life, he made 32 runs before he was caught behind. His performance was a disappointment to the crowd, who knew their hero was being watched by a county cricket official from England, and for Richards, who had on so many Saturday and Sunday after-noons lit up his club ground with the brilliance of his stroke play.

Richards recalls that day as if it were yesterday:

When people ask me about my love for Antigua, I give them this example. The whole crowd seemed to know that a man from

OPPOSITE The explosive stroke-making which caught the eye of Antiguans – and of Somerset's Len Creed (*Patrick Eagar*)

(INSET) The grim determination to succeed

England had come to see me bat. I could feel them wanting me to do well. And the umpire too, you know, he realised how important it was for me that I do well. Before I got many I was stumped off Underwood. He'd been out there playing some cricket. I went to drive, the ball, a quicker one, spun away and I was stranded, well out of my ground. I made as if to get back in, but didn't think I had. I spun round to look at the umpire, my heart was thumping. Then I realised that the umpire hadn't put his hand up.

Then when I got out a second time, with no reprieve this time, I felt I hadn't done enough to impress Mr Creed. What was worse was the fact that I knew all the players on the field knew that I had been given a life and I had failed to capitalise on the chance I had been given. I still had not made anything like a ton or anything like that. I had been too tense. I wasn't relaxed at all. And I felt the word would go round that I had been given a chance, everything was on my side and I had blown it.

One man who was not disappointed, though, was Len Creed. He had made up his mind that he was going to sign the young Antiguan for Somerset, and he called Colin Atkinson to tell him so.

Richards had been distraught at his failure with the bat. But he later realised that Len Creed had also been looking at his out cricket.

I think what saved me was my fielding. I used to field at cover point in those days and in that match I ran out a guy. I ran around from the covers and with only one stump to aim at, I hit the wicket. So Len Creed came to see me bat and I believe I managed to impress him with my fielding. That's why I've always believed that top players have to be competent in all departments of the game, not just batting or bowling.

Atkinson, on the other end of a transatlantic telephone line, tried his best to dissaude Len Creed from acting too precipitately. He argued that with three special registration players already on the Somerset staff, it would not be possible to sign up a fourth. What Atkinson didn't need to add was, especially if the fourth was an unknown Len Creed discovery!

Finally, a proposition was advanced, to which chairman Colin

Atkinson was unable to object. Creed suggested that he would personally bear the cost of getting Richards to England, that he would be responsible for the player's welfare while he was in England, and that if in the end Somerset decided to sign on the new discovery then the vice-chairman would expect to be reimbursed in full. If Richards was a failure, Creed would also bear the cost of seeing that the player was sent back to Antigua.

To say that this sudden course of events took Richards by surprise would be an understatement. Several conflicting thoughts raced through his mind. He had only just come around to the view, albeit very reluctantly, that perhaps the pursuit of a higher education in New York might be the only hope of improving his life in Antigua. Doing that, he would also satisfy the wishes of his parents.

The idea of a full-time career as a cricket professional in England had occurred to him, but his horizons were the Lancashire League and the possibility of playing for Oldham.

Arrogant though he was about his batting, he had remained, deeper down, a modest individual, who had dreamt of playing for his club and making runs for Antigua, even of turning the fortunes of Leeward Islands cricket, but never of representing the West Indies, by way of breaking into county cricket in England.

He was also very doubtful about whether he could live in England. The real joy of his life had been not simply playing cricket, but playing cricket in the warm, friendly, expansive atmosphere of St John's. He adored West Indian life: the non-stop parties around Carnival time; the informal drinking sessions at night which went on far in to the morning of the next day, and the people with their natural ebullience. With the odd job during the week and his cricket at weekends, Viv Richards in 1974 was a remarkably happy young man.

But Len Creed was persistent. He made it sound as though it had all been arranged. Although he nearly lost his young find when in attempting to dissuade Richards from joining the Lancashire League he mentioned the unforgiving cold of the English winter. That sharply reminded Richards that the cold in London, much further south, had been bad enough.

But now, there were decisions to be made. He discussed the matter with his parents, who deep down realised that the great city of New York was about to lose the chance of helping their son to become an electrical engineer, and with his club-mates, who were positive that

Antigua's time had come to break on to the stage of world cricket, with Vivian Richards and Andy Roberts.

Len Creed realised that he had not totally sold to Viv Richards the idea of exchanging his life in St John's for a new career in Taunton. So he kept in touch with the player, even when his West Indian tour with Mendip Acorns took him to the other islands and even when telephones were unreliable and the post was slow.

Creed's solicitude probably did more to convince Richards that the move was worth a try, perhaps far more than his father's eventual blessing and the encouragement of his friends. Remembering the difficulty he had experienced in making up his own mind, Richards recalls today that the terms under which he agreed to come to England after many days of agonising deliberations were quite extraordinary. It was, he says, remembering the risk Len Creed had taken, 'an arrangement based on faith and trust'.

Richards did not expect to drive directly from Heathrow Airport to turn out for Somerset on the following day. Len Creed had been scrupulously fair in explaining to him what the arrangement was. He'd play for a club in Bath, Lansdown, and from that launching pad he was expected to find his feet playing in English conditions and to do well enough to force his way into the Somerset team. It seemed the biggest gamble of Richards' life, but one he had decided to take. Once he had made that decision, Richards began to worry less. Unsure of many things, he was confident that he could bat. He felt it unlikely that any change of atmosphere would alter that basic fact.

Len Creed's interest went to the point of trying to ensure that he and Richards were booked on the same flight out of the West Indies. The fact that it had been impossible to do that caused a few anxious moments for the young Antiguan when he arrived at London Airport to confront immigration officials, without a work permit. But the problem was soon solved by Len Creed's intervention, and the star of Antiguan and Leeward Islands cricket was on his way to add his name to the Lansdown first team.

When he was not playing first-team cricket, he'd been taken on as an assistant groundsman. He brought to that job no more enthusiasm than he had earlier shown working in his cousin's motor mechanic shop in St John's, but, for a while, it kept him occupied and paid a small wage, enough to enable him to buy a round of drinks on Saturday nights.

Antigua, though, and the girlfriend, Miriam, he'd left behind, were never far from his thoughts:

'Everything about Bath made me miss Antigua. I missed the people, the music, the late-night ole talk about games. And I missed playing football on the beach.'

Life in Bath was certainly very different. Richards can now recall with humour things which at the time weren't very funny.

> This bit I'll never really forget. When I first came to the West Country I was put up with a guy from Barbados. This guy was the kind of West Indian who must have created the impression that he had a large house. All he had was one little room and the bit I was supposed to sleep in was where he kept his steel drums. I like steel drums a lot, but I didn't want to sleep with them. To make things worse, they would go out to parties and come back late at night, make a lot of noise and try to squeeze the steel drums into the tiny room where I was sleeping. For a long time that was Bath for me.
>
> Obviously if I was expected to be fit to play cricket, I couldn't stay in the room with the steel drums. So they fixed me up with some white people. The lady's name was Mrs Joan Oliver. They were a nice family and I became very friendly with one of their boys. We used to go to matches together. It made all the difference to have somewhere comfortable to live. Of course, I still missed Antigua, the sun, my friends and those lovely beaches.

Richards' love affair with Antigua and his attachment to his Caribbean roots were to remain the dominant and most powerful influence in his life.

In a perceptive and witty book, *Slices of Cricket*, the Somerset opening batsman, Peter Roebuck, writes of Richards:

> He'll chat endlessly about his days in Antigua, his years as a schoolboy, and the friends of his youth. Smokey's recollections are precise and hilarious. He holds his intimate audience for hours on end, and if he teams up with Joel Garner to chatter about olden times, the laughter will be uproarious – from the West Indians at least. No Englishman can fathom the lingo! At home in Antigua, Viv's house is open to guests, who range from the Prime Minister of the island to the dustbin man. All are received with the same grace.

Missing the West Indies . . .

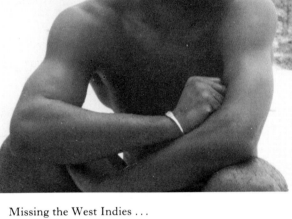

. . . and Miriam

And the thoughtful Roebuck makes this observation:

> Viv rarely gives vent to his strong views; his innermost beliefs
> remain hidden from all but his small circle of friends. Conse-
> quently his anger at injustice and prejudice surprises those who
> know only his ready smile. He has the presence, the personality
> and the discretion to emerge as an impressive and weighty
> ambassador for his colour and country.

Many years after Bath and Lansdown, caught in the political controversies of contemporary sport, his responses would always be
quietly and thoughtfully framed with the sensitivities of his countrymen in mind.

When Richards wasn't pining for his girlfriend, Miriam, or for
sunny Antigua, he was gradually beginning to learn that cricket can
be quite a different game in English conditions.

The famous West Indian allrounder, Learie Constantine, who
played for Nelson in the Lancashire League, was fond of recounting
how he discovered, to his chagrin, the degree to which the cricket
ball 'moved about' under leaden English skies. Getting under a

'skier' in the outfield, he'd been sure he had got right under the ball and was about to make the catch when he suddenly realised that the ball was falling several yards behind his left shoulder.

And the late Frank Worrell used to talk with great interest about the fact that his first priority when batting in England was learning to cope with the delivery which swung away late. There are some genuine seamers in the West Indies, but unless it's particularly humid, they can count on nothing like the 'late away-swing' their English counterparts are able to achieve. Richards was learning all this.

From his very first knocks for the Lansdown first team, he realised that the true hard tracks in Antigua were a thing of the past. Runs had to be made on damp, sometimes spongy batting surfaces. Throwing the bat at everything of a good length was hardly the recipe for the kind of long innings to impress the officials of the Somerset Cricket Club. What Alf Gover had attempted to teach him, those many months before at his coaching school in Wandsworth, suddenly acquired a pointed relevance. Hitting across the line of the ball could be a risky business in English cricket.

The other point of technique to be mastered was playing off the front foot. On hard West Indian wickets back-foot play was very much the order of the day. In England that was a little more risky. By listening to the counsel of his senior Lansdown team-mates, Richards adapted his style and in the process developed what was to prove one of the most profitable shots in his batting repertoire: forcing the good-length ball through the leg-side field, playing off the front foot.

Once he'd begun to get acclimatised and to adjust to playing cricket in Bath, the local club bowlers began to feel the raw power of Richards's unrelenting urge to hit every ball out of the ground. He was still getting out to lazy shots, still refusing to remember his father's advice to stay around and build a big score, but he was clearly in a class far above that of players on the local circuit. Very soon, his batting was the talking-point among players and officials in neighbouring clubs. Had it not been so, Len Creed would have spread the word himself. As it was, there was no need.

There is, alas, no rich fund of stories about how the young hero of

OPPOSITE Somerset opening batsman Peter Roebuck who listened to endless reminiscences from Richards and Joel Garner (ASP)

59

Antiguan cricket went in one astonishing leap from representing Lansdown to batting at number three for Somerset in Taunton. Richards admits that those anxious weeks before he joined Somerset were some of the more agonising in his life. Confident though he was about his cricket, and although he was beginning to enjoy life around Bath a little more, his future was still uncertain. On lonely nights in lodgings in the West Country, he would hear his father's words echoing in his mind: 'You could still make up your mind, Viv, and go to New York to study.' He felt sure that would be his fate if he failed to make the jump to representative county cricket.

His sponsor and mentor, Len Creed, had been doing his best. He had never ceased to impress upon his Somerset club officials what a magnificent chance they were about to pass up in securing the services of a great batsman.

Richards went to the Somerset nets and his batting was watched, silently and without comment, by senior players.

Richards remembers those days very clearly:

> At first I could only play for the under-25s. But that was OK for me. I was only too glad to play. You could imagine, it was a big step for me, man, to leave Antigua and to play cricket in England. I had never dreamt that would happen. My greatest encouragement came playing for Lansdown and making a few runs. What was great was that some of the teams we played against had the occasional county player or ex-county player and these guys were really good players. It was all new to me. The wickets were slow and they always seemed to be damp. But when I held my own in that class of company, I felt that I had a chance of making the big time. That was the really encouraging bit. So in those early days I was still raw, still learning, but growing in confidence, confidence in myself and confidence to play in different and difficult conditions. Some of the wickets weren't up to scratch and you had to play yourself in well and be very careful if you wanted to reach double figures. Any West Indian who wants to learn to play cricket in England, that's the kind of conditions he should be exposed to.

The young Antiguan found the older players very kind and helpful. And by now, with a career in professional cricket a distinct prospect, Viv Richards was anxious to recall all the things Alf Gover had sought to teach him.

Some of the older players were really very helpful. They would encourage you when things didn't go too well. I suppose they did see some potential in the way I played, you know, and they felt all that was needed was a little technique, a little more concentration. I began to appreciate the things Alf Gover had been telling me.

However, other overseas players were also in the running for places in the Somerset squad. Richards discovered this fact and became even more uncertain about his future.

The change in his fortunes, when it came, was the result not so much of any single great innings, but more the result of the constant verbal assault about how great a player Richards was, to which Somerset Cricket Club had been subjected. In the end, they could resist no more. Len Creed got his money back. Richards had been taken on to the Somerset staff.

In only a few weeks, Somerset too were to begin getting their money back. And to the glorious tradition of West Indian test cricket, a new star was about to be born.

Viv Richards won his county cap in 1974, a few months after he'd left Antigua. In what was left of that first season with Somerset, he scored a fine century against Gloucestershire at Bristol, and a few days later, returning to Bath, he got 107 against Yorkshire. Before the season closed, he scored 108 not out against Nottinghamshire at Trent Bridge in the John Player League.

Returning briefly to Antigua at the end of that first season with Somerset, his cricket had already begun to show a new maturity.

The Surrey off-spinner, Pat Pocock, tells the story of a Derek Robbins' eleven encountering an on-form Richards in St John's. Richards hit Jackie Burkinshaw for some eight sixes in going on to get 150-odd runs. Many of the bigger hits ended up in the churchyard at one end of the ground. When rain stopped play for a while and the umpires went out to inspect the wicket to see if play was again possible, Burkinshaw was heard to remark: 'Never mind the wicket, go look at the churchyard.'

Before he returned to England and his new club, Somerset, Richards' career took another step upward. He was selected to go to India for the West Indies. Right up to this day, Richards insists that the decision of the West Indies selectors to include him in the side to tour India in 1974/75 came as a complete surprise.

CHAPTER FIVE

*Earlier in his career Viv suffered from a little bit
of nervousness and did not make as big an impression
as we thought he was capable of. Despite all the
critics, I knew in my own heart that it was only a
matter of ime before this acorn grew into a big tree*

Clive Lloyd
West Indies captain

Richards had won his place in the West Indies team to go to India by virtue of his consistently excellent performances in the regional Shell Shield Tournament in the West Indies.

He was invariably among the runs. He'd got a fine 64 against a strong Trinidad attack in a match at Castries in St Lucia, and a few days later against Guyana he'd got into the 70s with a brilliant display of attacking strokes.

But he'd also begun to prove himself in that hardest of cricket schools, the English County Championship. And the word had begun to get around.

Towards the end of April 1974, he'd been given the Gold Award for his part in Somerset's match against Glamorgan at Swansea. He had been the major contributor to a match-winning partnership, rattling up 50 in no time, to set his team on the way to victory. His score of 81 not out contained one six and thirteen fours.

One week later Somerset had an emphatic win over Gloucestershire and, once again, Richards had been the man of the match. Playing superbly, he hit Proctor for 15 runs in his first over, put on a scintillating 112 with Denning and his score of 71 included one massive six and eight fours.

Hitting the ball out of the ground was, by that time, becoming something of a Richards' speciality. When the 1974 season closed, only Brian Close, of his Somerset team-mates, had hit more sixes than Richards.

Richards had begun to fulfil all that had been expected of him with

West Indies captain Clive Lloyd who helped Viv overcome his nervousness at the start of his test career (*ASP*)

extravagance. His first Sunday League 50 had come off only 40 deliveries. And on that fine summer's afternoon, he'd struck two mighty sixes in his very first over. Middlesex seemed to go on the defensive from that moment on, and Somerset won the game by a comfortable 16 runs. Later that evening, in the Middlesex dressing-room, with a fair sprinkling of senior test players around, the conversation had been almost entirely about Somerset's new young West Indian batsman.

But the young West Indian was beginning to learn very quickly that English county cricket could also be a severe test on a player's temperament. There were the high points, of course: with the season nearing its end, and batting before the Somerset home crowd at

Taunton, Richards had plundered the Surrey bowling, hitting a six and five fours to score 39, near the end of a limited-over game, and enabling his side to win the match comfortably by 8 wickets and with eighteen balls to spare.

But there were inevitably the struggles to get runs. In one particularly lean spell he'd got 9 against Kent, 4 against Yorkshire and, at a festival match against Lancashire at Torquay, where thousands had turned up to see him bat, he'd been bowled by Barry Wood for nought.

Throughout his career, Richards has stoutly maintained that batting records have never been a central preoccupation in his cricket, but at various times he's become terribly depressed when the flow of runs began to dry up.

In those early days at Somerset, the counsel of 'older heads' proved invaluable. For any instinctive player coping with lean times is as much a test of temperament as is batting on a difficult wicket. Accustomed to timing the ball perfectly and hitting it sweetly from the first moment he arrives at the wicket, failure to dominate an attack could quickly become a nightmare and thereafter a permanent loss of confidence.

Richards was repeatedly told by senior Somerset players that English county cricket was no picnic, even for the most competent batsmen. It took him a long time to come to terms with the fact that the vagaries of different county wickets made it impossible for any player to score freely every time he came to the crease. To the lessons he had learnt in the Caribbean was added a new injunction: he must learn to be patient, and he must be prepared to stay around long enough to build an innings, even when his timing was not there, and even when the wicket didn't make batting easy.

In that first season with Somerset the young West Indian was beginning to learn, the hard way, that batting was not all flair and brilliant stroke play. The one-time Somerset captain Brian Close, under whom Richards played, says that he had never met anyone in his entire career who was as anxious to learn as Richards was. The admiration is mutual. Richards has no time for those who describe Close as a 'bully' who talked and swore at his players if they didn't do as he wished.

He was no more of a bully than anyone else. Sure, at times there

OPPOSITE The extravagant drive through the offside field (*Patrick Eagar*)

was a lot of swearing and so on, and sometimes guys go over the top. But you've got to be prepared for that kind of thing. You can't get offended when you're pulled up, even if it's in a loud way. You must be open to criticism, however it is given, in whatever way. Professional cricket is no kindergarten.

Close describes Richards as 'modest, a good listener and quick to absorb the many challenges that English first-class cricket threw at him'. It was to prove extremely beneficial to him on his first overseas tour with the West Indies.

Going to India for the first time was a great experience. Incredible really. For a start, if you come from a small island like Antigua, the first thing to hit you is how big the country is. You travel hours to get from one part to another.

I had been selected to play for the West Indies when I was still trying to prove myself in the big company of the famous West Indies team. You know, it was a big challenge for me.

The other thing to hit you in India is the enthusiasm for the game. It was greater than I could have believed. You know, crowds of people around the team hotel every day. Hundreds outside waiting to see us arrive and leave the hotel and the ground. They would wait for hours. And many of them would just want to touch your hands if they can't get you to sign their book. It's amazing.

And when anyone reached fifty or a hundred or the score reached 200 or any kind of landmark, you know, the crowds let off firecrackers in the stand. It takes a little time before you get used to that. For a long time I thought bombs were going off or that somebody was shooting. But by and large, the Indian public is lovely. They are kind, hospitable, you have to keep turning down invitations if you want to play at all, and these people really know their cricket.

Next to a test series against England – the old colonial masters – West Indians take nothing in cricket quite so seriously as playing against India. There's good reason for this.

In Trinidad and Guyana there are sizeable East Indian populations. The 'Afro' West Indians were captured and sold on the West

OPPOSITE Richards' first encounter with the Indians was a disappointment. Later he learned to cope. Amarnath square driven for four (*Adrian Murrell*)

Coast of Africa and shipped out to the colonies through the dreaded 'middle passage' as slaves.

Indians, from the subcontinent, came to the West Indies as 'indentured servants'. Powerful humanitarian lobbies had suggested that the Indians were unsuited to prolonged periods of heavy manual labour in searing tropical temperatures. Their futures diverged. The slaves were slaves for life, kept in captivity until emancipation. Indian indentured servants served fixed terms in the employ of colonial plantation owners and were then 'paid off' when their periods of service were over. A common form of recompense was the gift of plots of land.

This gave the Indians an economic headstart over their Afro-Caribbean brothers. For a start, the Indians began to emerge as a landowning class and this led to no end of social and political friction between the two groups. It remains so to this day.

In Trinidad and Guyana for more than 40 years elections have been fought almost totally on a kind of 'racial' divide, between political parties or entities which appeared to represent 'Indian-Caribbean' or 'Afro-Caribbean' interests. This was certainly the undertone to the political battles in Guyana in the 1960s and '70s between Dr Cheddi Jagan and Forbes Burnham. The same can be said of Trinidad where the political antagonists during the same period were Dr Eric Williams and Dr Rudranath Capildeo.

This kind of division within the Caribbean countries, with its political and social fervour, bubbled over onto the cricket field.

When, during the early 1960s, Jim Swanton took a team to the West Indies, he frequently included (though I'm sure for no political reason whatever) one or two well-known Indian players.

On a visit to what was then British Guiana for a three-day fixture against what was then the 'colony' side, Swanton breezily announced on his arrival that neither of his two Indian players would be available for the match. Both players were indisposed. He was quite surprised to be told politely, but with the utmost firmness, that it would be most inadvisable to play a match in Guina, where some forty-eight per cent of the population was Indian, with neither of his two Indian stars. The point was taken and the Nawab of Pataudi was called from his sick bed to appear at the Bourda cricket ground.

The other side of the Afro/Indian division is just as amusing, although it undoubtedly has its serious vein. When the first Indian touring team came to Trinidad in the 1950s, people who had never before made the journey to the capital, Port of Spain, left their paddy fields and sugar plantations for the day to see the representatives of their mother country, India, play in the test match at the Queen's Park Oval. Much to the annoyance of some West Indian cricket supporters, the East Indians were vociferous in their support of V. J. Hazare's Indian test side. It was a strange phenomenon to be at a cricket ground in the West Indies where the support for the home team and that for the visitors was almost evenly divided. The Indian side had as much support as the West Indies have these days when they play against England at Kennington Oval in London.

So there's always some 'needle' to a West Indies visit to India and Viv Richards was aware of that as he flew east with the West Indies touring party.

The West Indians arrived in the subcontinent in early November and began the first match at Poona on 8 November. The West Zone side was not a bad one. Gavaskar opened with Naik, and Gaekwad Solkar, Joshi and Ghavri were also members of the home team. Carrying over his form from the English county season, Richards had a purple start. In his first game he scored a hundred. The wicket had been hard and true, the ball came onto the bat, and finding gaps all round the wicket, he stroked the ball beautifully to every part of the field.

The story of his first test match, though, was to be an entirely different affair.

The first test was in Bangalore. The night before the game was due to start there had been a heavy downpour. The West Indians were assured it was unseasonal and apparently it took the Indian cricket authorities by surprise. The pitch had not been covered. Clive Lloyd, reasoning that the wicket would only get worse as the match wore on, and realising what the magnificent Indian spinners could do in conditions like that, reluctantly decided to bat when he won the toss.

Given the conditions, the West Indians performed creditably on that first day. By stumps they were 212 for 2 and a West Indian celebration that evening was held to mark the fact that a young player, Gordon Greenidge, making his test debut, had scored a splendid 93.

Play on the second day was held up until after lunch by more 'unseasonal' rain. When a start was eventually made, Viv Richards and the rest of the West Indies batting walked into trouble, like lambs to the slaughter. The Indian spinners revelled in the conditions. They got the ball to bite and to turn and in the two hours after lunch the remaining eight West Indian wickets fell for a miserly 77 runs. The indignity for most of the West Indies batting lay in the fact that of that 77, Alvin Kallicharan had got 60 . . . the other seven batsmen had scratched together a miserable 17 runs. In the sorry pack was I.V.A. Richards. He'd holed out at mid-off, playing a clumsy shot at a ball that turned sharply. He'd scored four runs.

In the second innings, Richards fared no better. He again failed to read Chandrasekhar's spin and gave a simple catch to gully. That time he was out for three.

Richards was distraught at his failure. His first thoughts were of his parents and that multitude of loyal Antiguan supporters back home. He thought how they would have been following the progress of the game into the small hours of the morning. And he felt deeply for what he knew would be their keenest disappointment. He was totally dejected.

> I felt a bit low. When you leave a small place like Antigua and you know just how much all your friends want you to do well, it adds to the pressure you feel, you know. I thought of all those people listening to their radios and my constant feeling was that I have let these people down and I can't. Our third world people have very little to shout about and if you find yourself in a position where you represent what they are, how they feel as a people, my God, you can't let them down. Yes . . . I was under a lot of pressure to do well . . . for myself, for my family and friends and for the people of Antigua. That's the way it is.

Always loath to find any extenuating circumstances for his own failure, he refused to join in the fairly general condemnation of the Bangalore wicket. It had clearly been a monster, but Richards was convinced that his failure had been due mainly to his inability to cope. He has always felt that a good player must be able to bat well in any conditions. And he'd flunked the first real test of his mettle.

At the same time, Richards began to acquire a great respect for the skill of Chandrasekhar, the wily Indian spinner. Asked even today whether he's ever feared any bowler in the world, the name that is spoken almost with a kind of reverence is that of Chandrasekhar.

For the first time in his career he was finding it difficult to read the spin. Worse than that, Chandra made his well-flighted ball 'dip' so that even in pushing forward he could never be quite sure that the spinning ball was there to be hit, or even to be played quietly.

For a long time I just couldn't deal with Chandra: he flighted the ball so well. He also got bounce and turn. You'd make 30 or 40 runs against Chandra, but you could never be sure of getting him totally under control. Just when you thought you had got his measure, he'd produce the ball to deceive you. An incredible bowler.

Richards spent the interval before the second test in a state of considerable anxiety. It is perhaps a measure of the man that he seriously thought that perhaps he had overreached himself, and that somehow he lacked the real class necessary for the test arena. Until then he'd been enjoying India, seeing the sights and being swept along in a warm wave of kindly Indian hospitality. But his failure in that first test came as a great shock.

The West Indies, as a team, fared better than did Richards the individual. Despite their splendid spin bowling on the second day, India were beaten by a substantial margin. But for Viv Richards it was not a particularly sweet victory. His colleague, Gordon Greenidge, who had come so close to scoring a century in the West Indies first innings, made no mistake when the West Indies batted a second time. He set his team on the way to victory with a memorable innings of 107, thus joining that select band of players who have scored a century in their first test match. Richards' failure proved beneficial to him in one way. He acquired a lasting respect for some of the senior players in his team, particularly the captain, Clive Lloyd, who assured him it was only a matter of time before he was among the runs again. The team had also suspected that Richards was never happy unless he was belting the ball around. So, as he'd been told in Antigua by his father and by his schoolmaster, the senior members in the West Indies party were similarly advising him to play more carefully, to learn to 'build an innings' and not to try to belt every ball out of sight.

The Indian tour was to prove quite remarkable. For the first time in a series in the subcontinent, every test match was to produce a result, and India's defeat at Bangalore was not an accurate barometer of how the series would end.

Before the second test, Richards had two opportunities to regain a little of his confidence. Against the President's Eleven, he was out twice to the Indian medium-fast bowler Madan Lal, for scores of 16

71

and 9. Four days later, though, about a week after his miserable first-test showing, he was again in the runs scoring 103 and 53 in a country fixture. The West Indies had easily overwhelmed a vastly inferior side, but Richards hadn't been too concerned about the quality of the opposition. It had simply been marvellous to strike the ball in the middle of the bat after the nightmare of trying to 'read' Chandrasekhar.

The second test began two weeks before Christmas at Delhi. Immediately the wicket was again a talking-point: it hadn't been well prepared and batting on that first day was not easy. Fortunately for the West Indies, India were the first to make that discovery and by stumps on the first day they were all out for 220.

The West Indies began badly. Murray, the opener, went for nought, and Greenidge, one of the heroes of the West Indies first-test victory, fell caught behind, for 31.

Richards, usually so calm, unruffled and self-confident, approached the middle with the greatest trepidation. The easy, almost languid walk to the middle was there, but deep down his stomach churned with fear. He had decided that that innings was to be the most searching examination of his ability.

He got off to a very slow start, and had scored twelve when he was given the benefit of the doubt in an incident which might so easily have gone the other way, and plunged his career into a trauma of self-doubt.

Pushing forward outside the off stump, the ball went through to the keeper. There was an almighty shout from the bowler, wicket keeper and nearly all the Indian players. The close fielders were particularly vociferous. Richards remains absolutely convinced that he hadn't touched the ball. But the Indian players thought otherwise, and made their views known. But the umpire was unmoved and Richards stayed, breathing an audible sigh of relief.

The captain, Clive Lloyd, later walked down the wicket to encourage Richards that he should put the incident behind him. More to the point, Lloyd began to inspire his younger colleague by example. Using his height to the fullest advantage, he reached way down the wicket to smother the turn of the Indian spinners. He was merciless on anything short. For long periods, the West Indian captain treated the Indian attack with contempt, driving ferociously through the covers, rocking on his back foot and hitting the ball over mid-wicket or deep backward square and out of the ground. Gradually Richards' confidence grew. The main source of his inspiration was the way his captain played Chandra.

Richards carefully picked the deliveries to be put away, and after 90 minutes he was beginning to play with what, for the Indian bowlers and their supporters in the crowd, must have seemed like ominous freedom. His 50 was a relief and was generously applauded by the enthusiastic Indian crowd. Hitting the Indian spinners and medium-pace bowlers through the offside or forcing them through the gaps in the field in the mid-wicket region, he raced to his first hundred in test cricket. He hardly heard the firecrackers which the Indian crowd exploded in the stadium.

Relieved that he'd, in his own words, 'made it', he tore into the Indian attack with ruthless efficiency. He'd always believed that slow bowlers in particular must be made to feel the power of a batsman's shots. Richards feels it gives the batsman the psychological advantage and helps to force the bowler onto the defensive. So he drove the ball back fiercely to the Indian spinners. He wanted to make them aware of how hard he was hitting the ball, even when he didn't beat the field. The tactic worked. The Indian bowlers were soon in full retreat. Richards slammed his way past a hundred and fifty and batting by that time like a master of any kind of bowling and with all the confidence in the world, he was out eight short of a double century. To score 200 would have been a monumental feat. But to the man to whom records are no great prize, it didn't really matter. More important to him was the fact that he had proved himself in the big-match arena and his effort had shaped his team's victory in the second test against India.

The celebrations in Delhi that evening were no match for the spontaneous outburst of joy in far-away Antigua. By morning, the few hardy supporters listening to the radio commentary on the match at the Richards' home in St John's had grown into a jubilant crowd.

The most thrilling part of it all was Antigua's sense of pride in the achievement of its native son. Hear Lester Bird, Antigua's Deputy Prime Minister, describe that pride:

> ... if there was one innings that crystallised the superlative excellence of Viv Richards and endeared him to his fellow countrymen, it was his 192 in the test match at Delhi in the 1974/75 series against India. It was his first test century and the whole nation stayed up all night to listen by radio to this epic innings.

So, if any evidence was needed about why Richards had been so destroyed by his failure at Bangalore, there it was. He knew he had been carrying his little country on his shoulders, every time he went out to bat.

Mr Bird goes on:

With every run all our doubts disappeared, with every stroke all our anxiety subsided, with every boundary we collectively felt a sense of pride, of achievement and of togetherness.
    Viv Richards had made it. He had become a star and all Antigua glowed in the brilliance of his achievement.

The motivating force behind Viv Richards has always been his awareness that in playing cricket he carries the hopes and aspirations of much more than a team. Remember Mr Bird's earlier comments: 'Richards personified what we perceived ourselves to be: young, talented but yet unrecognised in the world.'

Having beaten the Indians convincingly in the first two tests, despite the problems caused by batting on wickets which were less than true, the West Indies had good reason to be confident that the series was as good as over. Not for the first time, that proved to be a costly miscalculation.

Perhaps West Indian confidence got the better of the team. Perhaps India were quite simply a far better side than the first two tests appeared to show. Whatever the reason, the West Indies were roundly beaten in the third test. Richards failed to get 50 in either of the two innings, and in the fourth test, although his fellow Antiguan Andy Roberts took seven wickets for 74 in a destructive spell of hostile fast bowling, the West Indies batted poorly and India coasted to victory by 100 runs. Richards' contribution had been a sound fifty in the first innings, but when the tourists' batting collapsed in their second turn at the crease, he'd failed to get into double figures. India had levelled the series two all, and there was one to play.

Two things stand out in Richards' memory about that fifth test: Clive Lloyd's magnificent double century, and the riot which followed, all because a few spectators ran onto the field to congratulate the West Indian captain.

The Indian police took a very dim view of the pitch invasion and

OPPOSITE A great partnership – Richards and Lloyd share a moment of triumph
(*Adrian Murrell*)

75

waded into the spectators with a heavier hand than authority dictated. The crowd didn't take too kindly to the way the police reacted and at one time the day's play was in jeopardy. The upshot of it all was that the West Indies lost nearly two hours, valuable playing time, in a deciding test match which showed every sign of ending up as a very closely fought game.

After a long consultation, the Indian cricket authorities decided against making up for lost time, and so nearing the end with only a marginal advantage, the West Indies were forced to have a go at the Indian bowling to get sufficient runs and at the same time to give themselves the opportunity to bowl out India. It was in this frantic dash for runs that Richards played a part: he threw his bat, hitting 39 runs off only 23 deliveries. Then a fine spell of bowling by Vanburn Holder, who took six Indian wickets for 39 runs, gave the West Indies victory and the series.

At the end of the tour Richards at last felt he was beginning to realise his potential. That was a good feeling.

> I would not have missed the experience of playing in India for the world. Of course I had to learn to cope with the Indian spinners. Even in zone matches out there, you meet bowlers you haven't seen before, who bowl something you haven't seen before and you have to be very careful. Otherwise you find yourself before a test match with no runs to your name in the run-up games. Those guys there turn the ball a mile even on those hard wickets. I learnt a lot in India. It's a great place to play cricket.

In February, a weary West Indian team travelled to Sri Lanka and Pakistan to round off the tour of the subcontinent. Richards wasn't among the big scorers in Pakistan, but took a century off Sri Lanka in Colombo.

By the end of the tour, Richards had scored four centuries: 192 against India in the second test, 151 against Sri Lanka at Colombo, 103 against North Zone at Jullundur, and 102 against West Zone at Poona. Only Roy Fredericks, of the West Indians, had scored more first-class hundreds.

The West Indies captain, Clive Lloyd, had been right all along when he said: 'I knew in my own heart that it was only a matter of time before this acorn grew into a big tree.'

CHAPTER SIX

*There was one notable exception as far as the West
Indian batting was concerned ... Viv Richards*

Wisden 1976

Richards' first overseas tour with the West Indies had been exhausting, mentally and physically. Enormous distances and long hours of travelling from one test match venue to another make a tour of India one of the more gruelling in a cricketer's experience. There was also the short trip to Sri Lanka and two test matches in Pakistan.

More than the physical demands, though, was the weariness which came of deep anxiety about whether he'd make it as a fully fledged test player.

Although his century in the second test had paved the way for his team's victory, and although he had distinguished himself as a fielder of superb athleticism and courage, he was unsure whether he'd done enough to retain his place in a West Indies team of stars. His ability to get runs quickly when the West Indies had needed to build a total worthy of an Indian chase, had pleased him. But he began to worry for the first time in his career about his ability to play spin. This alarmed him somewhat because he'd always believed that there was really no inherent difficulty in playing the turning ball. Batsmen, he believed, created too many problems for themselves. That's partly why one of his idiosyncrasies is that he never likes to be told by a batsman who's just been dismissed whether the wicket is 'turning' or not. He's also always felt that a batsman should approach the crease with a clear mind, uncluttered by the experience or failure of his predecessor. More to the point, though, unlike so many English players, he'd always felt that what a ball does in the air, or off the seam, or whether it spins or not, should be of little consequence. His philosophy to this day continues to be that once a player gets to the pitch of the ball, whatever the ball does should not be that much of a hindrance to playing a shot. Such is the philosophy of only the greatest of players.

After the Indian tour, he found himself thinking about technique for the first time. Alf Gover had told him repeatedly that he should use more top hand and left shoulder. He had seen the value of that in

From his earliest days Richards has been a fielder of athleticism and courage (*Adrian Murrell*)

his first season with Somerset, yet he felt he hadn't done as well as he might have in India.

As a result of these self-doubts, when the time approached for the West Indies to name their team for Australia, Richards was by no means certain that he'd be an automatic choice.

The Australian tour had come out of its regular sequence. The West Indies had not been due to go 'down under' for another two years. But, not for the first time, political considerations had intervened. Australia's intended tour of South Africa had been cancelled in a blaze of international controversy and the West Indies agreed to undertake the tour two years before they were due to go.

Richards was selected, but perhaps the idea of the tour was a mistake. For the West Indies Cricket Board, frequently strapped for money, it was a golden opportunity to have a share of the large Australian gates. But the performance of the West Indies led to the resurrection of that hoary old theory that West Indian cricketers are basically indisciplined and require the attention of strong-minded managers or brilliant, sympathetic captains, like Frank Worrell. The showing of the West Indians in Australia made it very difficult to argue convincingly against what is fundamentally an over-simplistic view of the way the West Indian plays the game.

Much closer to the truth is the shrewd observation of a West Indian poet:

When things goan' good, you cahn touch
we; but leh murder start
an' ol man, you cahn fine a man to hole up de side.

The team's performance in the first test in Brisbane had all the hallmarks of a Greek tragedy. No one would every explain what seized Clive Lloyd's team on that first morning of the first test against Australia in Brisbane. Even today, Richards' attempt at explaining what happened is hindered by his desire to put the nightmare behind him. Batting first, against the speed and terror of the Australian opening attack, the West Indians sent themselves hurtling to disaster.

The pre-lunch session was one of the most extraordinary ever seen on the opening day of a test match. In 18 overs, the tourists slammed and carved their way to 125. The point was, though, the West Indies had also in that period lost the entire top half of their batting. Six wickets had gone, many succumbing to the temptation to hook, so the cream of the West Indies' batting were back in the pavilion. Richards fell to Dennis Lillee for a duck and when the West Indies made their reply to Australia's first innings, he was run out for 12. The Australians won easily in Brisbane, although it must be said that the West Indies had been the creators of their own doom.

It is not one of Richards' happier memories. He says:

It's not very easy to apologise for any of that after all this time. But, quite frankly, I had never seen a wicket play that quickly in my life. And, of course, the Australian quick bowlers took full advantage of the conditions. It was an unbelievable scene. I was totally overcome by the whole occasion. To a large extent, some of our batting was pretty lousy. It all seemed to go to my head and I paid the price.

I played a bad shot in the first innings when I didn't get off the mark. It was pretty humiliating really. But five other wickets fell as well. I remember the scene in the dressing-room at lunch-time. None of the usual ole talk among the lads. Nobody tried to cheer us up. That was very bad really because West Indian dressing-rooms are generally a great place for jokes and there's usually a lot of noise. There wasn't very much though after that first session of the Brisbane test. There was no order. We didn't seem able to pull ourselves together. The whole place was in shambles. And let's face it, our spirits were down, we were down, we were very dispirited. I hope never to see anything like that again.

And even looking back on it now, you still think what a funny game cricket is. If we had taken the fight to the Aussie quickies and hit them out of the firing line, the outcome might have been different. But we tried and failed and paid the price.

Brisbane had been the worst kind of start for a touring side, and the tourists must have flown west with misgivings and not a little recrimination in their ranks. For the first time criticisms of the team leadership were beginning to surface. The Australian newspapers were later to make a great deal of the fact that Lloyd did not always appear to be in control, and when he did his decisions did not always make good strategic sense. The positively erratic and unpredictable approach of the West Indian team seemed even more evident in the second test at Perth.

Richards found his form before the second test, taking 175 off

Western Australia in the state fixture which preceded the test. But he failed to scale any such heights in the test match.

However, the West Indies, to the consternation of most Australians, won the Perth test handsomely by an innings and 78 runs, and with a full day to spare. If this gave rise to any thoughts that the West Indies were about to make a sustained comeback in the series, they were sadly wrong. The architects of the West Indies victory had been Andy Roberts, who took seven Australian wickets for 54 in their second innings, and Roy Fredericks, who scored a fine century.

The West Indies were roundly beaten in the third test, Richards again failing to get among the runs. Not that many others on the team did. The West Indians began to lose their self-confidence. Criticisms of Clive Lloyd's captaincy continued. He could do nothing right, and by the time the West Indies had gone down tamely in the fourth test, losing by seven wickets, due mainly to some excellent Australian pace bowling from Lillee and Thomson, morale had plummeted.

The West Indies had never won a series in Australia, but the memories of Frank Worrell's great tour – the Brisbane 'tie' and the 200,000 people who packed the Melbourne streets to bid the team farewell at the end of the tour – made the failure of Lloyd's team even more bitter.

The series did not improve for the West Indies, but gradually Richards began to find something of his old form. He faced Jeff Thomson for the first time, and was forced to adapt his technique to cope with a bowler who gave the batsman so little time to get into line. He found that the hook shot was not always easy against a bowler of Thomson's pace, even when some deliveries were just a trifle short. Whenever possible, Richards liked to hit fast bowlers straight back and over their heads. His theory is that shots like that are psychologically damaging to the bowler's pride, after which he is likely to present the batsman with a few 'gifts' in the succeeding deliveries. He did hit Thomson back over his head a few times, and all the West Indians hooked the Australian pace bowlers, Lloyd and Fredericks in particular. But in the end, Lillee and Thomson had the final word.

Sent in to open in a minor match of the tour, Richards batted beautifully to get 90-odd, and the West Indies, by this time shell-shocked and totally demoralised, quickly seized on this as a possible solution to their problems. The Richards part of the answer paid off

. . . the rest of the team, however, failed to do any better.

After the disastrous Sydney test, Viv Richards, opening the innings against Tasmania at Hobart, scored a hundred in each innings. He scored another century in the Adelaide test, and was out for 50 and 98 in Melbourne.

The West Indies had had the most miserable tour imaginable, but their failings had been put down squarely to their own unprofessional approach to the demanding business of test cricket.

Richards had been forced to think very carefully about whether his technique against the quickest bowlers in the world had been sufficiently sound, but in fact he was the only player to end the tour with an enhanced reputation. The great Australian players, Ian and Greg Chappell, said as much in interviews after the tour, and the terrible showing of his compatriots did not prevent commentators from talking about him as possibly one of the three best batsmen in the world.

In typical fashion, Richards had been concerned not so much about those occasions when he had scored runs, but about the countless times when his team could well have been assisted to greater things, had he stayed there to build a big innings. He left Australia resolving to pay more attention to getting his feet in the right place to play his shots. For his team, it had been something close to a massacre, but Richards left down under with five hundreds under his belt and an average for the tour of over 50. He says:

> It was my first really big tour and Andy Roberts was still green and just starting too. A few of our other players were up-and-coming also and perhaps it was wrong for people to have had such high hopes for us. But it was bad to lose so badly. Five-one is really terrible, you know. Really a terrible margin to lose by. But that made it nicer to be able to go back to Australia and restore our reputation and to win there for the first time.

Bringing forward by two years the West Indies visit to Australia had imposed the strain of an unbelievably heavy schedule on the team. After the drubbing in Australia, there was a five-test series against India in the Caribbean, with all the island fixtures in between, to be followed by an exhausting tour of England.

The England tour meant that Richards was unavailable for his county, Somerset, who were still struggling for their first title of any kind in their history.

The visit to the West Indies by India in 1976 was to be one of the more controversial of all time, in a part of the world where cricket is taken so seriously that it's sometimes difficult to prevent the friendliest match deteriorating into a storm of argument and mutual recrimination.

One commentator at the time wrote that when the Indian visitors left the West Indies at the end of the tour, they resembled Napoleon's troops on the retreat from Moscow. Nor would India feel that such a description overstated their plight. Some quite sensational cricket had been spoilt by controversy. And it all had to do with the West Indian fast bowlers.

Because, until very recently, they've never had many quick bowlers of their own, it had always been felt that against genuine speed Indian batsmen were suspect. On occasions, India's inability to cope with top-class speed had been cruelly exposed. In one most unfortunate incident in the mid-1960s, the Indian captain, Nari Contractor, had been hit on the side of the head during a tour and had to be flown to London for urgent medical attention. The Indians had never quite forgotten that incident, and had adopted the method of playing quickler bowlers by backing away to square leg. The West Indies fast bowlers then were Hall and Griffith.

For the 1976 Indian visit, the emerging names were Michael Holding and Andy Roberts. Roberts was fast and he had the ability to make the ball get up disconcertingly off a very good length, and Michael Holding, all elegance and silken action, was about the fastest bowler anyone could remember. He bowled the bouncer, of course, but his best delivery was the late away-swing. The batsman was invariably committed to playing a stroke less than worthy of the quality of the delivery.

The West Indies made no apology for having two of the fastest bowlers in cricket and were not about to tailor their attack to accommodate India. The selection of fast bowlers has always been a talking-point in the West Indies. And the position of West Indian selectors, team managers and captains is clear. West Indians have always felt that although they have, over the years, been asked to cope with hostile pace attacks – Trueman and Statham, Miller and Lindwall – for the most part uncomplainingly, if at times a little painfully, other test-match-playing countries began to complain of unfair tactics once the West Indies acquired pace bowlers of their own. There is a germ of truth in that. On one occasion, an Australian

Taming the Indian
bowling attack
(*Adrian Murrell*)

writer watched gleefully as Hall and Griffith destroyed the cream of the England batting, and wrote about the West Indies bowling in the most complimentary terms, only to make all sorts of accusations about 'unfair bowling' when it was Australia's turn to face the music.

Besides, the West Indies are, to put it mildly, terribly sensitive to any criticisms that they tend to over-use the short-pitched delivery. They are also unsympathetic, because West Indian top-class batsmen are all accomplished hookers of the short-pitched ball. And before the visit by India, the West Indies had only just returned home after a mauling by the Australian fast bowlers.

Apart from the controversy, though, one aspect of the series against India stood out above all else . . . it was the batting of Vivian Richards. In one of the most wonderfully consistent displays of high scoring since the great Everton Weekes, Richards scored a century in every test match, save the fourth. And even when he failed, he got more than 50 before falling to his old adversary, Chandrasekhar.

For the duration of the series, Richards' appetite for the Indian bowlers was insatiable. He cut and drove and hooked his way to a magnificent century in the first test against India at Bridgetown, paving the way for a West Indies victory.

In the second test match, before a capacity crowd at the Queen's Park Oval in Port of Spain, he got off to a very tentative start and for long periods was tied down by the Indian spinners. He reached his fifty after a little more than two hours, slow going for Richards, and was only 17 runs short of his hundred when he had the most extraordinary bit of good fortune. One of his Somerset team-mates has written that on a 'quiet day you stand a fair chance of running out Richards or his partner.' It was at such a point in his innings against India in Port of Spain that day. An accurate throw from Venkat left the Antiguan player hopelessly scrambling to make his ground. The Indian keeper, Kirmani, appeared to gather the ball, but then unaccountably failed to complete the stumping.

India paid dearly for that mistake. Richards went on the rampage to celebrate his good fortune. When he was eventually out he had scored 130, including 21 boundaries. The entire Oval crowd rose to acclaim the hero of West Indian batting.

The totally partisan manner in which the Trinidad crowd had claimed Richards as their own was clearly demonstrated when the West Indies batted in their second innings. The crowd was, by that time, beginning to believe that Richards was clearly invincible and when he was run out for 20, the spectators turned on Umpire Gosein. He was booed for the rest of that day's play.

The second test ended in a draw. The West Indies were therefore one up with two to play. The third test created its own slice of cricket history. India had what the statisticians regarded as an impossible task: they needed more than 400 runs in the last innings.

The barest details of the game are worth recalling. At one stage, the West Indies seemed to hold a commanding position in that third test. Although India sent back the first three West Indian players with only 52 runs on the board, in less than an hour and a half the West Indies recovered to end a scintillating day's play on 320 for five. The man who led the West Indian recovery was Viv Richards. He played a masterly innings of immense resourcefulness and authority. He cut and drove the Indian spinners and flicked the quicker bowlers off his pad with graceful ease. At the end of that first day's play, Richards had been left undefeated with 151.

India's reply was patchy. At times, they seemed capable of matching the home side's first innings tally, but eventually they fell short of their target of 359 by 131 runs.

Such a lead put the West Indies in good heart. Batting a second time, they did themselves no enormous favours, but their score of 271 meant that India were being asked to score over 400 runs to win the match, a feat which had never been accomplished in modern cricket.

India were sent on their way with a marvellously fluent opening stand by the diminutive Sunil Gavaskar and Mohinder Amarnath. Gavaskar got his century and Amarnath fell when he was only 15 short. Viswanath weighed in with a fine, controlled innings of 112 and Patel was one short of his 50 and undefeated when India achieved their historic victory, having lost only four wickets.

It was undoubtedly one of the more memorable matches in test match history. 'It was', says Richards, 'a great win for India. Gavaskar, Mohinder (Armanath) and Vishi (Viswanath) batted very well. We thought we had set them a high enough score and they made it. Our fans weren't very happy.'

The fact that the West Indies once again appeared to let an early advantage slip, as they had done in India two years before, might well have contributed to the anxiety and tension which surrounded the start of the fourth and decisive test match at Sabina Park in Jamaica.

There had been murmurings about an excessive amount of short-pitched bowling from the West Indies, but the umpires had said nothing and, in any event, the West Indian cricket authorities took these complaints in their stride. One of the reasons, perhaps, was the fact that the Indians have always tended to make the same accusations about West Indian fast bowlers. Commentators at the time recalled that the fast bowler Roy Gilchrist had been accused by Indian cricket writers of employing 'terror tactics' when he went on tour with the West Indies to India in the 1950s.

But Kingston was to be a far, far different story. Never before had a team made such a dramatic protest.

The first problem was that the wicket at Sabina Park was new and it proved to be terribly uneven. The bounce was not always true, at times it could be most awkward, and although Andy Roberts was suffering from a surfeit of competitive cricket and not in the side, Michael Holding was at his fastest and most hostile on the unpredictable pitch. Vanburn Holder was excellent in support.

India seemed well set to push the West Indies when they declared at 306 for six in their first innings. Even so, they might have done better yet, but for the fire of Holding. From 136 for 1, India had slumped to a score of 216 for 3, before the trouble and the controversy started.

Patel took his eye off a ball from Holder and the ball went from his bat to his mouth. Then Gaekwad, tall and determined, was hit rather painfully just above his left ear by a ball which quite clearly behaved in a very odd manner. It had jumped off a good length and, in attempting to get out of the way, Gaekwad seemed to duck into the ball.

The Indian captain, the gentle-mannered Bishen Bedi, was furious. He had been in no doubt that the West Indies bowling represented the worst kind of intimidation and he thought it appalling that the umpires refused to do anything about it.

Needing a very good score to put pressure on the West Indies, India's second innings began disastrously. Holding claimed the wicket of Sunil Gavaskar when he had scored only 2. After that, as the scoreboard relates, only two other players, Amarnath and Vengsarkar, reached double figures and five batsmen were recorded as 'absent hurt'.

India's scoresheet, or 'Bedi's protest' as someone called it, for that controversial second innings looked like this:

S.M. Gavaskar caught Julien bowled Holding 2,
A.D. Gaekwad absent hurt 0,
M. Amarnath stumped Murray bowled Jumadeen 59,
G.R. Viswanath absent hurt 0,
D.B. Vengsarkar lbw Jumadeen 22,
B.P. Patel absent hurt 0,
S. Madan Lal. by Holding 8,
S. Venkat bowled Holding 0,
S.M.H. Kirmani not out 0,
B.S. Bedi absent hurt 0,
B.S. Chandrasekhar absent hurt 0,
TOTAL 97 for 5.

In a way, it is not surprising to learn that Richards feels the Indian team made too much of their protest. He has no time for 'wingeing'.

> It wasn't that good a wicket. And the Indians felt that what Holding did, the way he bowled amounted to the fact that he was evil, you know. I think they took things too far. Holding was a young guy, he could bowl quick, he was keen and he was playing before his home crowd and anxious to do well. What didn't help Bedi and his team was the fact that the wicket was a bit on the quick side and there was a nasty ridge.
>
> The ball flew and flew fast and some of the Indian batters just couldn't get out of the way. I suppose players were bound to get hurt. I still think, though, that the Indian team made too much of a fuss. Cricket is a tough game and if a side is playing us they must cope with the pace, because we have some good fast bowlers.

It's an interesting comment on the spirit in which cricket is played that any bitterness caused after a test match like that one in Kingston is never long-lasting. Some years later when the West Indies were on tour in India, the services of Michael Holding and Andy Roberts were being anxiously sought to heighten interest in a number of additional benefit matches.

The biggest of these was to be played at the Wankhede Stadium in Bombay and the player most anxious to have the West Indian fast bowlers appear was none other than the former Indian captain, Bishen Bedi.

On 97 for 5, India were just twelve runs ahead of the West Indies.

And at first it had been thought that Bedi had declared his side's innings closed at that unlikely score. But to make his protest at the West Indies bowling even stronger, he said that he wished it to be recorded that India's innings had ended at 97 for 5. The match had therefore been virtually conceded to the West Indies and the series ended on a thoroughly bad-tempered note.

Richards was very disappointed at this. It seemed to cast a shadow over his most impressive test batting. By and large, the West Indies batting had been good, but Richards' contribution towered over those of his fellow West Indians: 142 in the first test at Bridgetown; 130 in the second test at Port of Spain; 177 in the third test at Port of Spain; and 64 in the final test at Kingston.

He had scored 556 runs for an astonishing average of 92.66.

Richards has always felt that his job for the West Indies is uncomplicated. He is there to score runs, he repeatedly tells himself, whatever the fortunes of the other members of the team. He had acquitted himself well in Australia, although the team hadn't. But to score runs in front of West Indian crowds and to play with such consistency, was more than he could have ever wished for.

I did feel really well you know. As a team we had lost in Australia, but I had not come out of it too badly. I had also done well against the Indians at home and that's a really good feeling. Naturally, it's great to get runs at Lord's or to make a ton in Sydney or in Melbourne, but to make runs at home in front of your own, that's the best. They don't have to follow the game on the radio, as they have to when you're abroad; they can actually be there while you make a few. And I had conquered the Indian spinners who had always bowled so well against me.

I saw a great deal of my parents again, and all my friends, had a few drinks with them. Life was looking great.

But there was always the next job, the next tour. We had just beaten India, but we were told in a very firm way, you know, that the next big challenge was ahead of us – our series against England. That was the series to win. I would say that that's the one our people seem most anxious to win and we were reminded of that. It's the killer series, the one against England. So, off I was again.

CHAPTER SEVEN

We was only *playin' de MCC, man;*
M-C-C
who come all de way out from Inglan.

We was battin', you see:
score wasn't too bad; one
hurren an' ninety-

seven fuh three.
The openers out, Tae Worrell out,
Everton Weekes jus' glide two fuh fifty

an' jack is de GIANT to come!
Feller name Wardle
was bowlin'; tossing it up

sweet sweet slow-medium syrup.
Firs' ball . . .
'N. . .o. . .o'

back down de wicket to Wardle.
Third ball comin' up
an' we know wha' goin' happen to syrup;

Clyde back pun he back
foot and prax!
is through extra cover an' four red runs all de way.

'You see dat shot?' the people was shoutin';
'Jesus Chrise, man, wunna see dat shot?'
All over de groun' fellers shaking hands wid each other

as if was they wheelin' de willow
as if was them had the power

Edward Braithwaite

'Wheeling the willow' against England has always given West Indian cricket teams enormous satisfaction, and a sense of great power. The converse is also true.

To West Indians defeat by England is seen as a national disaster of incalculable proportions. The pulse of the nation stops. West Indian pride dies in a torment of self-doubt.

It is as if any defeat by England is a signal that West Indian cricket fortunes are, from that moment, doomed to 'shallows and miseries'. And it hurts. Pride newly won is most easily affronted, as the former West Indies captain, Gary Sobers, discovered during the MCC's 1967/68 tour of the Caribbean.

Sobers' 'sporting' declaration in the fourth test match of that series in Trinidad allowed England to overhaul what should have been an impregnable West Indies position. In so doing, England won the match and the series, and within the space of an afternoon Sobers' fall from grace had been dramatic and almost total.

When he led the West Indies on to the field that afternoon he'd been a hero, the greatest West Indian player of all time. But when Cowdrey's team won the match Sobers had to be given police protection to leave the Queen's Park Oval.

The manner in which the incident developed is worth recalling in some detail.

The first test had ended in a draw. England's first innings total of 568 had been built around two excellent centuries from Ken Barrington and Colin Cowdrey. Although Lloyd's 118 gave the West Indies' reply a look of respectability, the rest of their batting had not been good enough to avoid the West Indies having to 'follow on'. In the end, the match was saved. England were in the ascendancy when the game ended but the first test ended in a draw.

The second test was also drawn, but with both teams on more equal terms. Both captains, Sobers and Cowdrey, contributed hundreds.

In the third test a resourceful century by the England opener, John Edrich, paved the way for a good first innings score, and a useful first innings lead against the West Indies. The West Indies had laboured over their response, in quite an 'un-West-Indian' way, at one particularly uninspiring stage scoring only 86 runs off 51 overs in about three hours. But Clive Lloyd came to the rescue of the home side with another century and the test match ran out of time.

The West Indies went into the fourth test without their two fast

bowlers. Wes Hall had been dropped and Charlie Griffith was out with a leg injury.

Rain spoilt the first day's play, but then the West Indian openers launched a fierce attack on the England bowlers. The first wicket partnership realised 119 runs before the Trinidad opener Joey Carew fell for 36. His partner, Steve Camacho, went on to make an aggressive 87 before he was out.

England's troubles weren't over. Nurse and Kanhai tore the England bowling to shreds: Nurse scored 136 and Kanhai made 157. With Lloyd hitting a quick 43 and Sobers scoring 48, the West Indies were able to declare at what should have been the totally secure position of 526 for 7.

England responded spiritedly. Boycott made 62, and Colin Cowdrey, all ease and elegance, stroked his way to a magnificent 148, before Sobers found a most unlikely bowling hero in the heavy-scoring Guyanese batsman, Basil Butcher. Butcher, whom no one had remembered seeing bowl in a test match before, took four wickets in his first three overs and ended up with the incredible bowling analysis of 5 for 15. At the end of the England innings he was applauded all the way back into the pavilion by his fellow West Indian players and by the large Queen's Park Oval crowd.

In their second innings, the West Indies went in search of quick runs and although Sobers had been without Hall or Griffith, he felt he'd done enough when he set England to get 215 runs in 165 minutes.

His plan to contain England, and try to win the test match by bowling them out, looked in danger from the moment England began their reply. Boycott and Cowdrey calmly and efficiently played their way to 55 off only 19 overs. And the score went from 73 to 173 in only another 18 overs before Cowdrey departed. Under the pressure of an England score which seemed to be inching ominously close to the target set by the West Indies, the great Sobers panicked.

His field placing was not as good as it might have been and with only a limited bowling attack to call on, he was unable to stop the England batsmen motoring smoothly on. For most of the time, Geoff Boycott was the image of solid caution. Playing defensively when forced to, he made few mistakes when he found gaps in the field.

OPPOSITE Colin Cowdrey. With Geoff Boycott, he was instrumental in drawing the 1967/68 MCC team back from the brink of certain defeat by the West Indies (ASP)

England reached their target with three minutes and a possible eight balls to spare.

The recrimination in the West Indies camp was bitter and long. There were reports that in the West Indies dressing-room Lance Gibbs, one of the more senior players, had rounded on his captain for having given England the match on a plate. It was also surmised that Charlie Griffith had found Sobers' tactics so generous to the opposition that he had decided not to make himself available for that crucial final session of the game, when Sobers needed him most.

> I have a lot of sympathy for a West Indies captain who finds himself in that position, says Richards. I wasn't playing then, of course, but I know how Gary must have felt. It is so much like what happened to us against India, and on that same ground too. It happened to Clive. We declared and set them over 400 to make, and they made it and they won. My God ... man, I've never seen people so angry. You'd have thought we threw away all the oil money in Trinidad. I find it very hard. No, I've never been able to cope with it. You toil your guts out, but you realise that to win sometimes you've got to take chances. If they come off, OK, but when they don't, man, people curse you like hell. That really turns my mind.
>
> It's a very funny way for people to behave. After a while you learn to live with it, but every time it happens it still shocks you. I just don't understand it. You learn to live with it, of course, but it's still a surprise when it happens. One minute you're on top of the world, and they're calling Hosanna in the highest. The other minute you're down, and they're all out there saying 'Crucify him'. It's a winner's world, ain't it?

The West Indies captain attempted rather weakly to suggest that he is a naturally attacking and adventurous player and that his policy had been to try to open up the game and to try to force a win, so that the fourth test would not end in stalemate as had the previous three.

Some English commentators, finding it easy to be magnanimous because of England's unexpected lead in the series, attempted to commend Sobers for his fresh and daring approach to the game.

None of this did the West Indies captain any good. Praise from the opposing camp tended to confirm that he had blundered. In the countless newspaper articles and editorials which followed in every part of the Caribbean, it was concluded emphatically that Sobers had recklessly gambled with the region's honour and had lost to England.

That night the world's greatest all rounder spent a lonely evening in his Port of Spain hotel room, with fierce arguments still raging among the West Indies players, while Colin Cowdrey was carried shoulder-high into the only 'English-style pub' in Port of Spain. The only person representing West Indies cricket at the England celebration was Bryan Davis, former Trinidad and West Indies opening batsman.

In the days that followed the débâcle of the fourth test, it was amazing to experience the fervour with which the head of the West Indies captain had been called for.

There was a respite of sorts while all attention switched to Guyana and the fifth and final test. Sobers redeemed himself somewhat, scoring 152 in his own dashing style. The West Indies had a first-innings score of over 400, but first Tony Lock with 89, his highest test innings, and later on Cowdrey, Barrington and Knott, frustrated West Indian attempts to capitalise on their sound batting and level the series in the final test.

The anti-Sobers editorials returned, this time pointedly accusing the West Indies captain of having handed England the test series for a song.

'If you lose in England, it'll go down badly at home,' Richards remembers manager Clyde Walcott saying before the West Indies left for the 1976 tour. It is difficult to imagine any West Indian expressing himself on the subject with such admirable restraint.

Richards had represented the West Indies in England before, although not in a full test series. He'd been a member of the West Indies team for the first-ever World Cup Tournament. The West Indies had swept past Sri Lanka, New Zealand, Pakistan and Australia to reach the final at Lord's, also against the Aussies. In an utterly absorbing day's play, during which the fortunes of both teams fluctuated, the West Indies overcame Australia to win the World Cup Tournament by 17 runs.

It had been a poor series for Richards, although in the final he hit the stumps on three occasions to get rid of Australian batsmen. But his batting had been well below par. He'd got 13 against Pakistan and Australia, and against New Zealand and against Australia in the final he'd failed to reach double figures. For him and for his side, the 1976 tour was to be a vastly different affair.

The West Indies teams which came to England in 1928 and 1933 had won only five of the thirty first-class fixtures. There hadn't been any appreciable difference in the fortunes of the side which toured England in 1939. The West Indian breakthrough came with the 1950 victory for John Goddard's squad, when the visitors won seventeen of their thirty-one first-class matches and lost only three.

Seven years later the West Indies lost to England, but when Frank Worrell led the West Indies back in 1963, his team won half the first-class games contested and lost only two. In 1966 and 1969, under Sobers, and in 1973, under Rohan Kanhai, West Indies' performances weren't as good.

Clive Lloyd's team, of which Viv Richards was a member in 1976, changed all that.

Of the twenty-six first-class matches played, Lloyd's 1976 team won eighteen, six were drawn and only two were lost. It was by far the best performance by a West Indies team ever seen in England. And the man who made it possible, and whose batting shone like the brightest star, was Viv Richards.

1976 saw the young Antiguan blossom into a player of world class. Graduation into this select band never comes before a successful run in England. In the 1976 England tour, Richards could hardly have been more successful.

In the 1930s the great George Headley had made over 2,000 runs on an England tour, ending the season with an average of 66.28. He'd played seven three-figure innings including an unforgettable 169 not out in the Manchester test match. Headley's outstanding scores on that tour were:

224 not out against Somerset at Taunton
200 not out against Derbyshire at Derby
182 against Warwickshire at Birmingham
169 not out against England at Manchester
167 against an all England Eleven at Folkestone
129 versus Glamorgan at Cardiff
129 against the MCC at Lords

In 1976 Richards did better. Due in the main to his batting, the West Indies slaughtered England in three of the five test matches. Richards

OPPOSITE Off to a flying start in the first test of Richards' first English tour (1976) (ASP)

missed the Lord's test, but scored 829 runs against England in the other four to end the series with an average of 118.42.

In all first-class games he scored 1,724 runs, for an average of over 70. His seven three-figure innings were:

291 against England at the Oval
232 against England at Nottingham
176 against Hampshire at Southampton
135 against England at Manchester
121 against Glamorgan at Swansea
119 against England at Scarborough
113 against the MCC at Lords

At the Scarborough match his 119 was built around one towering six out of the ground and 20 other boundaries, and won him the man of the match award. The West Indies won the second of the limited-over games against England at Lords to go two up in the series. Richards' score of 97 again gave him the man of the match award.

And the visitors completed the rout of England, winning the third match by 6 wickets.

By the time the tour ended the batting of one player had become inextricably linked with the fortunes of an entire team. Few other players in the history of the game have exerted that kind of profound influence. Richards enjoyed every minute of it. At times, he was almost too kind about participating in the celebrations which seemed to accompany his every great innings.

A telling example of this came during the Oval test against England. With 130 not out to his credit at the end of a day's play, Richards was kept up until half past two the following morning by the non-stop West Indian party in his hotel room at the Waldorf in the Strand in London's West End.

Richards remembers the evening well. But neither he, his West Indian colleagues nor his Somerset friends will make a guess at how many people crowded that room, although at about eleven o'clock in the evening there were certainly 30 people or more. The hard core was undoubtedly made up of Richards' relations in London. But the son of the Prime Minister of Antigua was also there, and so was a good proportion of the Antiguans living in London.

One Somerset club official found it extremely difficult to understand this West Indian lack of concern for the welfare of a player who was required to carry on batting the following day.

The same official is absolutely sure that when Richards went for 291, failing to make an assault on Sobers' 365, which many had expected of him, he was out to a tired stroke, due in part to the fact that the celebrations the night before had deprived him of a good night's sleep.

Richards later made the point that he had not been terribly concerned about 'cracking' Gary Sobers' record. And one must take his word. The view of one of his Somerset friends, who watched the party the night before with some astonishment and dismay, was that Richards might have found it difficult to summon up the energy to have a go at getting 365, even if he were so minded. But he would never turn his West Indian compatriots away from his door. They were keen to share in his triumph and he was anxious to share his joy in its abundance with his people. It is that that gives him great satisfaction. He is always close to the mainspring of West Indian pride. And he is keen to proclaim it.

> I feel that we in the third world [a theme he constantly refers to in his more thoughtful conversations], who do not have a great deal to shout about in material terms, should take a pride in what our people achieve. And if you do well in one particular job, playing cricket or so, it's nice to let the brothers share in your achievement. Sure I was a bit late that night, but that's a small price to pay for giving your people a good time. And you mustn't forget they were around to congratulate me. So it was nice for me as well. In any case I hardly ever go to bed much before midnight, even during matches. The thing I hate if you turn in earlier is to wake up very early in the morning and not be able to go back to sleep. So I prefer to go to bed late and sleep right through until morning.
>
> That night at the Waldorf was different to my usual routine. I would usually see a few friends, go to bed just after twelve, having read myself to sleep with *Time* magazine or *Newsweek*. But I had scored a hundred and was not out and my people wanted to help me celebrate.

He saw his success in 1976 as an extension of the general feeling among the West Indian players whenever they took the field at Kennington Oval. Looking around at the thousands of West Indian faces in the crowd, the message from the senior players was: 'We must not let these people down.'

It was Deryck Murray who I first heard say that as we were going out to field. And I think he and Clive used to make sure the players were aware that although they were playing cricket, they kinda had a wider responsibility. You know, you think of many of those West Indians in England who live such dull, uninteresting lives. A win by the West Indies changes that and they walk around with their heads high, you know, because we did well in the field.

It was Somerset's good fortune that Richards' form stayed with him for the 1977 county season. He'd been sorely missed the year before, but now he was back to make up for his absence with an abundance of glorious runs and scores of match-winning performances.

Those Somerset fans who were also supporters of England during the 1976 test series, had comforted themselves as Richards destroyed the England bowling with the thought that it would be only a matter of time before he returned to do the same for Somerset. In the eyes of many, he had only been 'borrowed' by the West Indies in 1976, and really, his primary assignment was with the county of his adoption. At least, they reasoned that England had been subdued by a 'Somerset man'!

So much had his popularity grown even by 1977 that thousands of people would flock to the ground, not so much to see the match – although they were keen to see Somerset win – but to see the great Viv Richards bat. When his innings ended, it was always possible to observe a quiet exodus from the ground.

Few left unsatisfied during the 1977 English County Championship season.

The dominant feature of that season was the batting of Viv Richards. By the time it ended, he had become known as 'King Viv', the 'terror of Taunton'. One of his team-mates, none other than the great Ian Botham, talked about Richards' 'incredible reflexes, his ability to pick up the flight of a ball, his unselfishness in always playing for the team rather than for himself'.

Ian has always been very generous about my game. I think we have a relationship based on mutual respect. But selfishness

OPPOSITE One of the joys of playing for Somerset – the company of the irrepressible Ian Botham (ASP)

100

cannot enter into a team game like cricket. You know, it's eleven players in a side. They all have a job to do, but it's for the team as a whole. I want to play well and make runs because that is my job. But I want to do well not just for Viv Richards but because I'm playing for Somerset or for the West Indies.

In 1977 Somerset won six Championship matches and in nearly every single game Viv Richards led the way. He barely failed to reach 1,000 runs in the County Championship fixtures alone, and his average was 86.

His striking rate for the entire season was an astonishing 50 runs per hour, some indication of the fact that no bowler or county attack worried him unduly. Caring little about run-ups or styles, whether a bowler came over or around the wicket, whether he used the crease or not, Richards, his head still and eyes fixed on the bowler's arm, pulverised most attackers who had the misfortune to meet him in a run-getting mood.

In that memorable season, his tally of runs in all competitions was 2,874. That included three double centuries and five centuries. He had fourteen other scores of 50 runs or more.

Without much argument one of his most remarkable innings that year was the one against Gloucestershire at Bristol. Somerset had not had a good match and were facing defeat when Richards came to the crease. He batted throughout the day to save the match for his side, and at stumps he was undefeated with 241 runs to his name.

Against Warwickshire at Taunton on 1 June, he'd hit two sixes and eleven fours in his first knock and when Somerset batted a second time, Richards resumed his onslaught against the Warwickshire bowlers. In two and a half hours he struck sixteen fours and two sixes to make 118.

His double century against Surrey at Weston-super-Mare gave him his 2,000 runs for the season and the added pleasure of seeing his friend Peter Roebuck get his first century for Somerset. Richards and Roebuck put on 251 runs for the Somerset fourth wicket, Richards went on to make 204, including five sixes and thirty-five fours, and Surrey were overwhelmed by 158 runs.

In another County Championship game at Taunton, he batted with a cracked fingerbone, but still managed to score 70 runs in 65 minutes. In his county's John Player League match against Gloucestershire on 28 August 1977, and before the home crowd at Taunton, Richards was again in tremendous form. Gloucestershire had begun briskly by scoring 33 runs in their first nine overs, but their pace faltered a little and their allotted 40 overs produced only 127 runs. Even so, no one quite expected Somerset to win the match by nine wickets and with five overs to spare. That such a result was achieved was due almost entirely to an amazing innings by Viv Richards.

Rose and Denning gave their side a sound start putting up 56 in the first sixteen overs. When the first wicket fell 'King Richards' took charge.

Unluckily for Gloucestershire, they missed stumping him before he had got into double figures. Their bowlers paid heavily for the lapse, none more so than the off-spinner, Graveney. In one brilliantly savage burst, Richards took 34 runs off Graveney in one over. His team-mate, Peter Roebuck, writes that: 'Viv Richards does not always attain ... fierce majesty, but when he does, he bats with fury ... that is Richards at his greatest, utterly determined to destroy an attack.'

That's how he was that day against Gloucestershire, utterly determined to destroy an attack. In the space of twenty-four minutes he'd struck one six and five fours in his 62 runs. Luckily for Gloucestershire, that was sufficient to win the game for Somerset, for had Richards been forced to bat any longer, his opponents might have had a far sorrier tale to tell.

His Somerset colleague makes this analysis of Richards' batting, from the point of view of someone who was watching him from the other end of the wicket a great deal during that incredible 1979 season.

'Richards can bat with skill and even technical perfection if he so desires.' Roebuck asserts that Richards can defend his wicket 'with prodigiously careful forward defensives;' although 'he is so good, he does not need to defend on bad wickets. That is why he only plays long defensive innings if he is in a particularly impish mood.'

And as for those hazardous mid-wicket drives from off-stump, which Richards employs with such devastating effect, Roebuck feels that bowlers should not always believe that they could get Richards out by tempting him into that particular indiscretion. 'For a long time,' says Roebuck, 'the bat comes through the line of the ball; only at the last minute do steely wrists deflect its trajectory to find some yawning gap through the legside ... Nowadays even accurate away-

swing bowlers are reluctant to aim at off-stump or anywhere within reach ... Richards does look fallible; there's just a chance he might decide to hit the next ball over extra cover, or maybe he'll charge down the wicket with nothing particular in mind ... Batsmen as aristocratic in their splendour as I V A do not always quite understand that while he feasts on boundaries, others must scavenge singles.'

In 1977 Richards feasted on a surfeit of boundaries.

His contribution to Somerset's County Championship chase was:

118 against Warwickshire at Taunton,
241 not out against Gloucestershire at Bristol,
104 against Leicestershire at Leicester,
204 against Sussex at Hove,
101 against Warwickshire at Edgbaston,
189 against Lancashire at Southport,
204 against Surrey at Weston-super-Mare.

In addition, he scored 104 against Derbyshire at Taunton in the John Player League.

After his exploits for the West Indies against England during the summer of 1976, Richards had had a lean period with the bat. In five test matches against Pakistan, which began in the West Indies later that same year, he had scored less than 300 runs and had not once made a hundred. But his form had begun to return when he got 143 playing Sheffield Shield cricket in Australia for Queensland.

So that by the time he reported to Somerset in the spring of 1977, he was ready for the fray.

That season Somerset failed to win any national cricket honours, but no one felt they would be too long a time in coming. Not with the extravagant talent of Viv Richards in the Somerset side.

But while Richards had been breaking the heart of bowlers throughout that 1977 season, the very foundations of the international cricket establishment were shaking with the news of a revolutionary cricket programme, which threatened to change the face of the game in the foreseeable future.

West Indian players were drawn to the Kerry Packer cricket experiment because it was based on paying a professional cricketer his worth. Given the way cricket developed and is run in the West

OPPOSITE 'Richards *can* bat with skill and even technical perfection, if he so desires' – Peter Roebuck

105

Indies, the West Indies Board quickly realised that they were powerless to try to stop or to destroy Mr Kerry Packer's enterprise. They quickly realised the futility of attempting to arrest a movement to which their own players had given such allegiance.

Unfortunately, the West Indians were unable to convince the other members of the International Cricket Conference that they too should refrain from the costly effort of trying to 'kill off' Kerry Packer. Had the wisdom of the West Indies authorities carried the day, international cricket might have been spared some of the turmoil and trauma of what came to be known as 'the Kerry Packer Affair'.

English and West Indian cricket bosses had vastly different perceptions of the Packer intervention. The English cricket authorities felt that players who opted to join the Packer cricket tour had somehow betrayed a sacred trust; whereas the West Indian Board saw that Mr Packer was offering West Indian players the financial security which they had always sought – and which they had never been able to find in the West Indies.

Thus while the English and Australian authorities angrily resolved to 'punish' Mr Packer and his players, the West Indies Board moved to limit some of the damage to West Indian cricket that could be caused by the Packer alternative.

The allure of the Packer enterprise was simple: professional cricketers were, for the first time, presented with a choice. Cricket had found an alternative sponsor and some of the best players in the world decided to go with the alternative – among them, Vivian Richards.

CHAPTER EIGHT

We felt that to take what appeared to be retrospective
legislation on players and penalise them . . . was not moral

Peter Short, West Indies Board,
on the 1977 ICC ban on Packer players

Professional West Indian cricketers are, in the kindest sense of the word, mercenaries. Deprived of the opportunity of playing for their livelihoods in the West Indies, they must sell their services to clubs in England and in Australia. It's a fact of life.

The West Indies Board pay their players to represent the West Indies in test matches, but for almost nothing else. Thus the Board effectively has no prior claim on the services of West Indian players. Neither does it attempt to force a claim on those services.

That's why for Viv Richards, his captain Clive Lloyd and the other West Indians who joined Mr Packer's World Series Cricket, the decision to do so was about the easiest one they'd ever made.

Mr Packer offered his players an opportunity to achieve a measure of financial independence. He offered them money. In so doing he was addressing what might be called the dual concern of the vast majority of players: how to earn a living wage during their comparatively short active playing years and how to survive when their playing days are over. Mr Packer was offering enough money for players to begin to believe that both those things were possible, perhaps for the first time in cricket history. He was also telling professional players that they were worth much more than they were being paid by the official cricket authorities.

The problem has always been particularly acute for West Indian players. At the end of their playing careers, they usually depended on the fact that they were sufficiently well-known to be given positions in large corporations, or they forced their way in having acquired some academic qualification along the way.

Learie Constantine, for instance, spent an agonisingly long time after his cricket ended reading for the Bar, and was later employed by an oil refining company in Trinidad. Frank Worrell read Economics at Manchester University and worked at the University of the West Indies in the years before his tragic death. Clyde Walcott went into industry, and Gerry Gomez and Jeffrey Stollmeyer retained connections with companies they were involved in throughout their sporting careers.

But it's not always that easy. Wes Hall returned to the West Indies after an illustrious playing career and was only very luckily rescued by a coaching contract from a big tobacco firm. Roy Fredericks and Rohan Kanhai were for a time given Government assignments to do with cricket, but a large number of players, even the great Gary Sobers, was never assured of continuing employment on their return to the Caribbean.

This experience formed the backdrop to the decision of the West Indies Board that it would be morally indefensible to penalise players who were only taking the best offers around at the time.

Mr Packer's representatives approached Viv Richards and the other West Indian players during the second test match against Pakistan in Port of Spain. A few weeks later, the international cricket authorities held a series of meetings to decide how to deal with what they saw as an undisguised threat to established cricket.

The manner in which the West Indians Alan Rae and Jeffrey Stollmeyer failed to convert the other members of the International Cricket Conference to their point of view is worth recalling in some detail.

The very first formal meeting to discuss the Packer development, the Test and County Cricket Board's (TCCB) Advisory meeting, set the tone for what followed. The chairman referred to a letter from Sir Donald Bradman which apparently expressed grave concern about Mr Packer's World Series Cricket and linked its birth to Ian Chappell's 'long-disclosed wish to upset the applecart in Australia'.

The former England captain, Peter May, made the sensible observation that so far as he knew, the Test and County Cricket Board had no hold on players outside the English county season.

A few days later, ten days after Mr Packer's plans became public and some three months after Viv Richards had signed his Packer contract, the chairman of the TCCB first raised the possibility of banning Packer players from any future participation in test cricket, or of banning them from county cricket at the end of their contractual county agreements. This second possibility was later to terrify some English county officials who saw Mr Packer's adventures during the

English winter as having nothing to do with the availability of their players for the summer. In fact, almost the first thing Viv Richards did on signing his World Series contract was to assure Somerset that his playing in Australia would in no way affect his commitment to the club.

When the Test and County Cricket Board met in early June 1977, the Derbyshire representative urged his colleagues to try to understand why the players had decided to play for Mr Packer. Having talked to some players, he said the general view had been that Mr Packer was making a commitment to players' interests far more than the TCCB had ever done. He suggested that the TCCB should take a more constructive approach to the Packer affair and try to 'extract maximum advantage from it'.

But the Leicestershire representative disagreed. Switching the discussion to what should be done to players who signed for World Series Cricket, he pronounced: 'I would not have them in test cricket, or even county cricket.'

The Test and County Cricket Board decided that no approach should be made to Mr Packer for 'peace talks' before a full meeting of the International Cricket Conference in mid-June.

Bob Parrish and Ray Steele represented Australia, and Harold Burnett and Allan Rae came to speak for the West Indies Cricket Board. Jack Bailey attended as ICC secretary and W.H. Webster took the chair. Australia's tough anti-Packer line dominated the meeting. Mr Parrish suggested that the ICC should do all in its power to fight 'private promotion of cricket', insisted it was not time to 'co-operate with Packer' and said that players must be made to choose between playing what he called 'Board cricket' or 'professional cricket'. In his view, they could not play both.

The meeting finally framed a resolution to be put to another I C C meeting on 26 June. Should a solution not be found to the Packer problem, the meeting should declare that:

No commercial matches should interfere with test matches or other first-class cricket; any outside promotions must provide money for cricket as a whole.
Therefore:
Players contracted to Mr Packer should be given the opportunity to draw back from the brink. Any player who plays for Mr Packer ... should be banned from test-match cricket. With

109

regard to English players currently involved with Mr Packer, such bans should apply from the end of the 1977 season.

The West Indies spokesman at that meeting, Allan Rae, had been constantly urging caution while these declarations of righteous indignation were being drafted, but his reservations had been pushed aside. The general tone of the meeting was expressed by one speaker who declared: 'Wars are not won by appeasement.'

During the course of the June meeting of the ICC, Jeffrey Stollmeyer and Allan Rae urged the reopening of talks with Mr Packer. He said that he had raised the matter because of what he saw as 'the terrible consequences of confrontation'.

Stollmeyer then went on to say that his Board was not entirely in agreement with the proposed changes in the TCCB rules to ban Packer players. He said that a different consideration applied in the West Indies, adding that none of the West Indies players who signed Packer contracts was under any contractual obligation to the West Indies Board. Stollmeyer said his Board felt that it would be wrong to ban players retroactively. He felt it might make more sense to ban players as and when they became unavailable for domestic or international competitions.

Stollmeyer's colleague, Allan Rae, followed this exposition by reaffirming his Board's sympathy with what the ICC was trying to achieve, but he insisted that West Indian players who signed Packer contracts had breached *no* agreement with the West Indies Board. They had not, he said, even breached a 'disapproval rule'. Therefore, Allan Rae argued, the players had entered into 'legally binding contracts at a time when we did not disapprove and when they were not under contract to us'.

Rae went further. He told the meeting that the West Indies Board had in the past discouraged governments in member countries from 'banning players retroactively for playing matches in South Africa'. The West Indies Board, faced with several West Indian governments determined to take such a firm line against racist South Africa, had spent much time persuading them to bar only those players who had known of the rules in advance and then gone on to break them. It would then be strange, Rae argued, if the West Indies Board itself was to decide to ban players who had done nothing more than sign a contract to play for a private promoter – a contract which was legally binding and which did not cut across any prior arrangement with the West Indies Board. 'We will take action against our players', said Rae, 'when they are unable to play for us.'

It was a powerful encapsulation of the case of the West Indies Packer cricketers. It was also a prudent way to proceed.

Still, many of the other ICC members persisted in their calls for 'war' against Mr Packer. One Australian representative said that privately-promoted cricket à la Packer should be: 'nipped in the bud, and the sooner the better.'

In the end, the West Indies, having failed to persuade their ICC colleagues to adopt a less-militant posture to the Packer tour, announced with regret that they would be unable to vote for the banning resolution. And Allan Rae hoped that any press statement made after the meeting should clearly state what the position of the West Indies had been at the meeting.

Had Allan Rae had his way, it might have made the West Indies Board's later dealings with the West Indian Packer players a little smoother. As it was, the West Indians were persuaded that it would be inadvisable to tell the world how any single member voted, and the meeting heard a little speech from Mr Hadlee of New Zealand in praise of unanimity. He urged the West Indians to support a resolution that they felt to be morally wrong, in order to save the ICC's image.

After lunch Jeffrey Stollmeyer said that the West Indies had been forced to 'weigh the moral implications of our responsibility to our players against the need for unanimity.' They were voting for the banning resolution, but asked that their reservations be recorded in the minutes of the meeting.

Needless to say, these reservations were never disclosed until the decision-making process of the ICC had been laid bare in the High Court. Despite the West Indian volte-face (in the interest of 'unanimity') Allan Rae ended with this submission. He repeated his view that the banning of players was morally unfair. He warned his colleagues that to ban players retroactively could land the ICC in court because it meant declaring that the contracts the players had entered into were illegal; and he said:

We feel that we are giving Packer a weapon to fight this conference. He is offering players a lot more than they were earning. Most countries will henceforth try to ensure that players earn more. Players were free to enter contracts. But when they did, we penalised them. Who will be considered fair . . . we . . . or Mr Packer?

Despite Allan Rae's final plea, Mr Hadlee of New Zealand, unmoved by arguments of morality or fairness declared:

'I believe our public image depends on the public announcement we make. We must tell them why we acted as we did and why Mr Packer is wrong.'

That was the crass bunker-like attitude which resulted in the ICC having to pay out a small fortune in court for embarking on an illegal course.

By the time the court case had been decided in Mr Packer's favour, the 'circus', as the group had been disparagingly called, had already assembled in Melbourne to start its series of games.

Of the West Indian players, Viv Richards had by far the best of that first season with World Series Cricket.

The fact that he got runs, on wickets which were being prepared in a revolutionary way, came to be regarded almost as a justification for the experiments. Playing under floodlights and with white balls proved to be, in Richards' view, a commendable innovation. Nor did he find the cricket lacking in competitiveness. The Packer cricket pitted Viv Richards against some of the toughest competitors in the world. To this day he remembers his clashes with Len Pascoe, who reacted with such incredulity when Richards repeatedly hooked him into the pavilion and smiled, the tigerish Rodney Marsh and the talented Chappell brothers. He found the going extremely tough and never ran up the high scores he had earlier for Somerset. He did get 99 not out at Perth playing for the West Indies against Australia, 79 in his first 'Super Test' – acclaimed by many as one of the best innings they had ever seen – and 177 for a World Eleven against Australia.

Richards had never harboured any doubts about joining Mr Packer's World Series Cricket, even when he was the centre of some controversy about whether he had other commitments in Australia which would prevent him from signing on.

It would be naive to pretend that the West Indian players were not

OPPOSITE, ABOVE LEFT The change from all-white cricket clothes was only one manifestation of a cricketing revolution

ABOVE RIGHT Playing under floodlights was another

BELOW The effect was spectacular, but highly controversial (*all Adrian Murrell*)

attracted to Mr Packer's scheme, primarily because they were going to be well paid for playing cricket. But Richards makes the point that there was another powerful reason:

> If a guy has a plan to bring together all the best cricketers in the world, then if you feel you're any good you want to be included. It's part of the prestige of being a good player. From the start I had no doubts about it.

And the cricket was tough:

> For a start, the Packer people gave us long talks about what being a professional means. And they were dead serious. We had to be fit and you had to play to the top of your ability. There were incentives, you know, prizes for players who did well in a match and it was hard going.
>
> The Australians are the toughest people to play against. They will talk to you before a match and be very friendly and so on, but once the game starts it's daggers drawn. They behave as though you're the world's worst enemy. Nobody plays it quite as tough as they do and that was part of a great experience. Players like Rodney Marsh and Ian Chappell, and Lennie Pascoe would try to outstare you and even insult you when you're at the wicket, you know call you names and tell you what awful shots you play, and you have to be able to stand up for yourself. It's a hard school playing cricket in those conditions, and Mr Packer had made it possible.

Frowned on by the Australian cricket establishment, Mr Packer and his associates were forced to play some matches at venues which had never been used for cricket. Wickets had to be 'manufactured' or 'grown' in special conditions and then transferred to the match venue with due ceremony and a great deal of care. This part of the Packer plan was also widely criticised at the time. Viv Richards feels that they were some of the best wickets he's ever played on:

> The wickets were very good. The fact is, runs were not easy to get. Players knew they were taking part in a brand new thing which everybody didn't approve of, so everyone was trying hard.
>
> I enjoyed the night cricket. Cricket must progress and that is what Mr Packer tried to do. We had no personal quarrel with the establishment. We just wanted to take part in this great new

experiment, where all the best players in the world were. It's easy to laugh at the white balls and different coloured cricket gear and all that, but what's wrong with it? Bowlers were still out there trying to knock your head off, giving no quarter and I as a batsman was still trying my best to score runs. I had these clashes with Lenny Pascoe. He tried to intimidate me and it was up to me to show him that I wasn't afraid. He didn't like it when I hooked him out of the ground. But unless you take the attack to a bowler like Pascoe, he gets the better of you. It's either him on top or me. I decided if I had to survive, it must be me.

The inevitable clash with the West Indies Board came when the Australians toured the West Indies in 1978. Australia, minus the cream of their talent who were banned because of their Packer commitments, were easily beaten by the West Indies in their first two tests of the series.

For the Guyana test, the West Indies Board decided to drop Haynes, Austin and Murray. There didn't seem to be much logic about it, except that the West Indies were under constant pressure to do something about their Packer players. Until then, they had been the only test-match-playing country who had not banned their players involved in World Series Cricket. The West Indies captain disagreed with the decision of the selectors to drop the three players and said he would not lead the team under the circumstances. Richards and six other West Indian players joined their captain in the walkout.

Some elements in the West Indies Board saw the incident as a naked attempt by the West Indian players to take over the administration of the game. 'Player power' is how it was described at the time, and a common view was that West Indian players had grown too big for their boots after the Kerry Packer controversy.

Given the enlightened attitude of the West Indies Board during the decisive London meetings about Mr Packer's World Series Cricket, it was sad to see the Board dragged into the mire of the ensuing controversy.

Having warned the International Cricket Council about the dangers of banning players, the West Indies Board now found itself under pressure to take action against Packer players. In deciding to drop three players, the Board probably had in mind some token gesture, some compromise which would be seen as falling short of seeking an open confrontation. But the senior West Indies players felt they had to make a stand of principle. Once the West Indies captain, Clive Lloyd, had decided on a course of action, Viv Richards was totally happy to go along with what had been decided.

> The key to my reaction was that I trusted Clive. We had played the first two tests in Trinidad and Barbados. Then, to our surprise, the selectors decided to drop Murray, Haynes and Austin who had played so well and who hadn't failed or anything. We found it hard, you know. Our decision was taken at an emergency meeting chaired by Clive before the third test in Guyana. Andy (Roberts) and I were in Antigua and we didn't go to the meeting, but Joel (Garner) kept us informed of what was going on by phone. So he phoned up and told us what Clive and the guys had decided and once they'd made up their minds about what we were to do, that was it. All we needed to hear was the advice of the skipper and we stood by him. It was a complicated business, of course, but in the end our decision wasn't all that difficult.

Richards was terribly disappointed not to be able to complete the series against Australia at home, but he was determined more than ever to continue playing World Series Cricket.

Before that, though, after a short rest in Antigua, it was back to Taunton for the 1978 English County Championship season.

Because Richards drives himself so hard and because his commitment to his game is so total, disappointments, either personal or team, are all the more acute. For Somerset 1978 was to be a season of bitter disappointment. Neither was it to be a brilliant season for Viv Richards.

Somerset finished fifth in the County Championship, second in the John Player League, were Gillette Cup finalists and were semi-finalists in the Benson and Hedges. Everything so near and yet still so very far away from their first-ever trophy.

Essex were also in search of their first major trophy in 1978 and of the four teams left in the competition, fate cast Somerset and Essex together. By the time the game got underway, for the Gillette Cup semi-final, the Taunton ground was bursting at its seams.

Somerset won the toss and decided to have first strike. The departure of Phil Slocombe first ball provided a hint of the drama to come, but no one took too much notice. Somerset's number three was the towering figure of Viv Richards. Richards descended the pavilion

116

Six 'Somerset men' in test: Richards and Garner for the West Indies; Rose and Botham for England; the umpires neutral

stairs fairly quickly, but then began his slow almost indolent walk to the middle. Even at moments of the greatest tension, it's the most casual stroll in cricket, the walk of a man unworried by whatever the opposition can throw at him.

Happily for Somerset, Richards was on tremendous form. He launched a fierce attack on Lever, Phillip and Pont. He streaked past his 50, as his assault on the Essex bowlers continued. As he had done to Derek Underwood in the final test against England at the Oval two years before, he hit Ray East over extra cover for six, although the ball had pitched on middle and leg and was a perfectly good delivery. Richards' hundred was inevitable. He was finally out for 116. More significantly, from his team's point of view, he had helped Somerset from their score of 86 for 2 to 189 before the third wicket fell.

Only Peter Roebuck of the other Somerset players really got going. He scored 57. Although Essex bowled steadily but without brilliance,

Botham was bowled for 7, Burgess for 5 and at the end Vic Marks was undefeated with 33. However, a score of 287 for six in 60 overs was not to be regarded lightly. And Essex would have to bat well.

They began almost as badly as Somerset had. Denness was caught out before his team had reached double figures. Graham Gooch appeared in superb form. He is one of the hardest hitters in the game and can be virtually unstoppable when he's batting well. Gooch got 61 before he fell to Joel Garner, but Fletcher's 67 and Keith Pont's 39 kept Essex in the hunt. When the seventh wicket fell for 248, Somerset might have been excused for feeling that the match was as good as won.

It was to turn out much closer than that. Turner and East sneaked a few boundaries between them and suddenly Essex needed 23 runs in three overs. Turner fell, leaving the fray to East and Smith, and 13 runs were required in the final over. Five came off the first two balls, and the third bowled East, but it was a no ball. An overthrow gave Essex three more runs and they required only four more from two balls. Going for the winning run, Smith was barely caught out of his ground after a heroic scramble by two Somerset fielders and the scores were tied at 287, giving Somerset the victory because they had lost fewer wickets.

Richards and his team were to remember that scoresheet for a long time:

Somerset
  B.C. Rose caught East bowled Pont 24,
  P.A. Slocombe lbw Phillip 0,
  I.V.A. Richards caught Denness bowled Gooch 116,
  P.M. Roebuck caught Lever bowled Phillip 57,
  I.T. Botham bowled East 7,
  V.J. Marks not out 33,
  G.I. Burgess b Lever 5,
  D. Breakwell not out 17,
  Extras 28.

  TOTAL (for six wickets in 60 overs): 287.

Essex
  M.H. Denness caught Marks bowled Dredge 3,
  G.A. Gooch caught Taylor bowled Garner 61,
  K.S. McEwan bowled Burgess 37,

K.W. Fletcher caught and bowled Botham 67,
B.R. Hardie run out 21,
K.R. Pont run out 39,
N. Phillip run out 1,
S. Turner bowled Botham 12,
R. East bowled Dredge 10,
N. Smith run out 6,
J.K. Lever not out 5,
Extras 25.

TOTAL (60 overs . . . all out): 287.

Three weeks later the bottom fell out of Somerset's world: they lost two finals in the space of forty-eight hours.

They were beaten at Lords in the final of the Gillette Cup and then met Essex again in the final of the John Player League. Essex had scored 190 in their forty overs, thanks mainly to a sturdy 76 by their captain, Keith Fletcher. Somerset lost two wickets with their score on 18 and always struggled after that.

Richards was so dissatisfied with his performance (he gave an easy catch to mid-wicket off the bowling of Gooch, when he'd scored 26), that he smashed his bat into a hundred little pieces in the Somerset dressing-room. He probably sensed what was about to happen. With his departure, Somerset were 69 for 3. Roebuck and Botham took the score to 87 before Roebuck went, and Botham's 45 gave his team a fighting chance. But the last six batsmen could only muster just over 50 runs among them and Essex won the John Player trophy by two runs.

No one who follows Somerset cricket will ever forget that traumatic weekend. Talk to Viv Richards about those two trophies lost in the space of two days and his recollection pours out in a stream of words:

It's funny, but I have a feeling that that sort of thing will never happen to us again. When I think of what really happened, I think we just got carried away. We told ourselves, here we are, we have reached the final and we have done quite well. But the important thing is that perhaps we never had the real confidence in ourselves to take it further. We were happy to have got to the final and that was that. I think we are more mature now. I know we are. And in any case, since it happened to us before, we will know how to approach a similar situation.

About his own performance Richards says:

> I was a bit tense, I must admit. I didn't play my normal innings: I was tentative; I was being too careful. I didn't want to be the one to throw it all away and I knew the team was depending a little bit on my batting. So I blame myself, for not relaxing more and playing the shots I normally play in county matches. But then sometimes you don't, do you, when you're in your first big final and we were so keen to do well for the fans, you know.

Losing one final was bad enough. Trying to summon up the courage to play the second required a superhuman effort. He says:

> Could you imagine, trying to pick yourself up and to give a hundred per cent for a second final after losing the first one? At least this one was at Taunton, but it was hard to know whether that was good or not because you had to face the fans. Those loyal people had been built up to such a high and you know we thought they had a right to feel that maybe we had let them down. They must have had such a terrible drive back from London. Ours was so sad and awful.
>
> I think when it came to the Sunday game at Taunton, some of us wanted to slip into the ground without anybody seeing. And then when we came to the ground we couldn't believe what we saw, you know. We got to the ground very early and it was absolutely packed. I just couldn't believe my eyes. Many of the people seemed to be in the same clothes they wore to London the day before and they were just as enthusiastic. There was a hum of excitement and expectation around the ground. Unforgettable really. They were giving us encouragement as we came into the ground and it was all very emotional. Hardly anyone in the dressing-room spoke, although we had to try to pick ourselves up from the disappointment of the day before in London.
>
> And then we lost that game too. I found it very hard to take. I had been on losing sides before, but never like this. Two finals in two days, both lost, and it felt very sour. Man, I tell you, back in the dressing-room grown men were crying. I put my hands in my head and I broke down and cried. I just couldn't help it.
>
> But what really moved me was the people, the supporters.

You know, those people who had travelled and lost with us, who had been lifted up and brought down with us – those people wouldn't leave the ground after the match. They stayed and stayed, and they had to to see us because we didn't want to come out from the dressing-room to face them. And then came the really emotional part. The fans gathered in their thousands in front of the dressing-room and they called every player by name, until that player came out onto the balcony and the applause was incredible. When they called my name and I came out on the balcony to tremendous shouts from the fans, I broke down again. It was so emotional, man.

What moved me was the attitude of the Somerset fans. There were no insults, you know, no recrimination, like when you lost a match in the West Indies. These fans still wanted to pat you on the back, to shake your hands and to say 'Better luck next time'. And they were right in a way. We lost this time, but we were a young team, we were just beginning to put it together, to go places. Joel and I and Ian were all young and we needed time to put things right as a team.

Our team had a great schooling under Brian Close when he was our captain, and we were bound to come good some time. But it would have been understandable if the fans didn't understand that, having been so let down. But those people were so nice. They had faith in us. They knew we would come good some time. And they just clapped and shouted as though we had won. No team had ever been so well regarded by its fans in defeat. It's the greatest tribute I can pay to the people of Somerset.

Understanding though the Somerset fans were, the fact remained that the club had come close to success and had blown it. Failure at the last two hurdles had cast a long shadow of disappointment and gloom over the whole season. Nor had Richards been at his best. His major scores – 118 against Sussex, 110 against Leicestershire at Taunton, 139 against Warwickshire and 116 in the Gillette Cup semi-final – represented a tally far below his best. His first-class average for the season was just over 45.

Whenever he failed to get among the runs, Viv Richards worked at his game. And if he felt his technique had not been at fault, he resolved to work on another aspect of his game.

121

Richards is almost obsessive about physical fitness

He was becoming obsessed with physical fitness. He would turn up at the Somerset ground in Taunton a couple of hours before the other players, to put in several laps around the ground. Then he would do pressups for half an hour before the game.

One Somerset player painted this picture of the team dressing-room before the start of a limited-over Sunday game: Richards doing endless pressups in one corner of the room, while in the other sits Ian Botham, smoking a cigar and reading the *News of the World*.

Richards drives himself hard, and is as tough in his judgment of his fellow players as he is on himself. Sitting in the players' enclosure during a test match in Bombay in November 1983, he loudly remonstrates with a player who fails to grasp the opportunity of taking a quick second run and mutters to himself with sharp disapproval: 'Too many damn cigarettes.' At times like these, Richards gives the impression that he would never do anything which would stand in the way of his one-hundred-per-cent commitment to the game.

And when Malcolm Marshall plays an airy shot outside the off stump and gives encouragement to the Indian attack, with the West Indies still needing more than a hundred runs to overhaul India's first innings score, Richards gesticulates angrily: 'What kind of bloody shot is that Maco, for Christ's sake?' he asks with a rhetorical flourish. One feels it's just as well that Marshall is a long way off and cannot hear the anguished cries of a perfectionist.

There's something of this too, in the preparation before Richards leaves the team hotel to go to the ground.

He is awake just after seven and will listen to the radio or put on his tape recorder, depending on where he is in the world, before having a shower and ordering two large glasses of fresh orange juice.

After a shower he combs his hair, applies a variety of skin creams, takes vitamin E with tissue salts when it's likely to be very hot, sometimes another tonic vitamin, and bathes his eye before setting off for the ground.

He moves about the room with a casual air, but goes about his preparation with deliberate care, making sure nothing is forgotten. A stroll down to the hotel lobby to join the team bus on time is usually accomplished with headphones on and reggae or calypso music blaring in stereo. He exchanges a few remarks with his team-mates and then settles down in the back of the bus, sinking deep into the seats and into his music.

By the time he reaches the ground he is relaxed and raring to go.

CHAPTER NINE

Our people have been bought and sold throughout history.
I don't care whatever anyone else does – I will never play
cricket in South Africa. One must have principles

Viv Richards

Viv Richards has been offered the equivalent of one million dollars in Eastern Caribbean money (about a quarter of a million pounds) to play cricket in South Africa. And that was only the latest in a long line of similar offers, which began well before the annual 'rebel' tours became such a cricketing talking-point.

The last offer, like all the others before it, was met with a polite but firm refusal.

The Antiguan cricketer who likes to boast that he doesn't want to get involved in politics, and who tells interviewers 'I am a cricketer, and politics is a dirty business, no matter what side you're on,' is, in fact, intensely conscious of political reality. He may genuinely frown on purely party politics, but he is deeply concerned about the status of black people in the world. He speaks with uncontrollable anger about prejudice based on race, and despises the South African system of government, which, in his mind, institutionalises the 'degradation' of the majority black population.

In the summer of 1976, when he missed the West Indies second test against England through glandular fever, he was contacted by phone on his sickbed by a South African journalist who enquired whether he'd accept eighty thousand dollars to play club cricket in the Republic.

Three years later, a South African hotel chain flirted with the idea of promoting a multiracial team tour in South Africa. The nucleus of the team – and the prize personalities as far as the South Africans were concerned – were to be Viv Richards, Clive Lloyd, Joel Garner and Collis King from the West Indies, and the dashing England allrounder Ian Botham.

Apparently, a part of the deal was that Richards be deputed to sound out his friends in the Antiguan Government to discover

With daughter and fans at Worcester

whether the tour would meet with approval at West Indian government level. Although the tour was scheduled to last for a mere three
weeks, the fee per player was well in excess of eighty thousand
American dollars. Richards refused to even mention the idea in
official circles in Antigua and has been reported as saying some time
later: 'That kind of money goes to show you that things are not really
right. They were trying to make money talk.' He added: 'I've never
been to South Africa and at the present moment I won't go. I've
spoken to whites, blacks and coloureds about South Africa and the
result was two to one. So the whole affair was over. I won't go until
they clear up the racial inequality.'

Richards is openly scornful of the argument that it is possible to
separate the fundamental nature of a government from its conduct in
ancillary fields, such as sport. He is therefore inclined to the belief
that sporting contacts with South Africa can never be right while the
black majority in that country lives under the oppression of apartheid. Token attempts at integration in some sports leave him singularly unimpressed.

His attitude to those players who decide to play for large sums of
money in South Africa is unambiguous: he will defend to the death

125

a player's right to make his money where he can. Cricketers must do what their consciences allow, he says. He still retains a warm friendship with the Barbadian player Gregory Armstrong, who was one of the West Indians who signed up to play a number of games in South Africa in 1982. Armstrong has been a friend and remains one. During the 1983 season the young Barbadian was Richards' guest at Taunton. Armstrong had been slightly concerned that his presence at a county fixture, when Richards was leading Somerset, might be an embarrassment to the Antiguan. But Richards insisted that if Armstrong felt like spending two days in Taunton, he was quite welcome.

Nor does Viv Richards condemn the so-called English 'rebel' cricketers. He said:

> Goochie and the others made their choice and, man, I'm not going to wear a black armband every time I play cricket against them. It's up to each cricketer individually to say which is the right way to fight against apartheid, and the white players aren't in the same position as we are.

Adding his personal opinion of their action in playing in South Africa, he says:

> But having said that, I think it was a mistake them going. They were used. They were used to make the South African system look better. It was blood money, and in my mind they shouldn't have taken it.

He relates with wry amusement that one of the West Indian players who went to play in South Africa, Barbadian Collis King, has since found it difficult to look Richards in the eye when they meet.

And, like most West Indian players, Richards is not over-impressed with the attitude of his former West Indian colleague, Alvin Kallicharan. He refuses to publicly challenge Kallicharan's decision to go to the Republic, but he is quite contemptuous of Kallicharan's stated views about apartheid. In a television programme about sport in South Africa, Kallicharan volunteered that he had been thrown out of a Wimpy Bar and the Rosebank Hotel in South Africa. Asked how he felt about that, the Guyanese batsman replied: 'I was wrong to go there.'

To put it mildly, Viv Richards would find it intolerable if he were fussed over, applauded and paid large amounts of money for his prowess on the cricket field by day, only to discover that later that same evening he was excluded from a Wimpy Bar because he is black.

He believes that if he put himself in the position where he couldn't go to a Wimpy Bar because he is black, it would be a grave insult not only to him but also to his country and to his countrymen. He says:

> How would I explain to people in Antigua, that I went to play for money in a country where I and all my friends would be second-class citizens? It would be immoral for me to go to South Africa, because if I went I would, within certain restrictions, live like I do in Taunton and Melbourne or here in St John's. I'd live that way in South Africa because I'd be used. I'd get special treatment and I don't want special treatment. Once I packed my bags and left, what would it be like for the other blacks and coloureds in South Africa?

Told about the news that his former West Indian colleague Colin Croft had been turned out of a 'whites only' railway carriage in South Africa, Richards is wide-eyed and shocked. He remains incredulous, as he asks about the incident in all its detail.

Croft, playing for the 'rebel' West Indian team in South Africa in the 1983 season, was on a train from Cape Town to a suburb where the West Indies were playing a match as part of the two-month tour. A ticket collector approached him and requested that he move to a car set aside for 'non-whites'.

A white man who had been sitting next to Colin Croft and who had been talking to the player, protested and encouraged Croft to stay put. At the same time he tried to explain to the ticket collector that Colin Croft was a famous West Indian cricketer and was in South Africa on a highly publicised tour as a 'guest of the Government'.

The inspector listened impatiently and then brusquely insisted that the West Indian should move to a 'suitable' carriage.

Listening to the story, Richards is silent. His countenance saddens and there's a flash of anger as he shakes his head in disbelief. He is told of Croft's response to this incident. Croft had been quoted by the news agencies as saying that he had been 'happy and willing to move' and that it was 'no big thing'.

Richards repeats that West Indian phrase to himself. 'No big thing.' He sticks to his policy of not publicly criticising his fellow West Indians who have gone to play for huge sums of money. But he is really shocked by the Croft story.

'How the hell could a man subject himself to that kind of shit?' he asks, not really expecting an answer.

'I am not sure how things work here,' Croft had been quoted as saying.

'Bull, man, bull,' says Richards, clearly angry that a West Indian and a former colleague in the side had been subjected to such humiliation.

'How the hell could I look Antiguans in the face?' he asks, 'if that sort of thing happens to me?'

For the next two days, before the preoccupation of other things take hold, the Croft story is thoroughly dissected in the West Indian team.

The West Indian players aren't famous for the subtlety of their political judgments, and by the large they observe the code of not openly condemning what any one of their number has done. But they have harsh words for the South African system. Attempts at reasoned condemnation soon break down into curses and expletives. Richards continues to mutter under his breath. It is clear, although he does his best not to express the thought too openly, that he blames Croft for putting himself in a position where his dignity as a man, as a player and as a West Indian could be so affronted.

What he is more forceful about is a system which finds it impossible to disguise its true nature even when it is desperately trying to put on a respectable face to a critical world.

Man, you would have thought those people could arrange things a little better. After all they want people like Croft to play there. That's a rotten system, man. It's no good for me as a black man. I couldn't play there while things are like that. It would be impossible for me, you see. I wouldn't want to be treated like that. And I wouldn't want their special treatment either. So until things change, I'm not sure I could make that scene.

Richards has given a great deal of thought to the controversial issue of whether players who go to South Africa should be banned. 'Bans are not for me to lay down,' he says, 'because I hate to condemn a guy for making his living. Also I think it's a rigmarole, saying you can't play cricket with South Africa while other people are trading with it. Yet, the more I think of it, bans helped to create pressure on South Africa and let their government see that the apartheid system is not working. In the end, though, nobody from the outside will change the system. They'll have to do it themselves.'

Growing up in the Caribbean when he did – at a time when West Indian governments were attempting to shake off what they saw as the shackles of colonial rule – Richards is acutely aware of the political aspirations of his countrymen.

Their struggle for self-determination encouraged among their young a belief in contemporary black liberation movements. Richards identified with the American black power movement. He has, perhaps, never totally embraced the philosophy, but he sympathises with its general aims and would hear no intellectual arguments against it. To his way of thinking it was the drive for black self-assertion and equality of status which provided the base for the American civil rights movement. He feels that the battle cry of the American black power movement (led, incidentally, by a West Indian, Trinidad-born Stokeley Carmichael) corresponded to his country's aspiration to assume full responsibility for its own political destiny.

Talking to Richards about his views on South Africa or about black liberation movements as seen from the perspective of the black West Indian, one realises that the force of his beliefs springs not from any intellectual coherence or well-structured arguments, but from the need to identify. He has arrived at what he believes not because he has made a careful study along the way, but because the need to identify with contemporary West Indian causes pointed unerringly in one direction. He is a child of modern West Indian thought.

Thus, he would say that he is an admirer of the late Haile Selassie, the Ethiopian leader, who came to be venerated by some West Indians as something of a spiritual guru. At times in his native Antigua, Richards, driving around in his car, would point to a picture of Selassie on the dashboard and say, 'He's the king around here you know.' In the same breath he would swear undying allegiance to the Selassie movement.

But if he is ever tested on precisely what that belief is, he would broaden the discussion and it would emerge that his allegiance is based not so much on what Haile Selassie did, but on the fact that his high profile in the arena of third world politics popularised certain causes. For a time, Selassie's name (at least in the eyes of his supporters) gave prominence to certain black points of view. In

Richards' own words: 'He made the people of the third world, people like us, realise that there are greater things to be achieved in this life and that it's worth struggling for.'

Richards himself feels a desperate need to identify, without too much involvement, with that brand of third world message. Moreover, because he has, by his cricket, achieved an international profile, he believes he owes it to his compatriots to publicise their cause.

Defining that cause in its philosophical entirety is difficult. It's almost easier to say that it's against racism. It's against any thought that the contemporary West Indian is not able to scale the heights in twentieth century society. It's for black self-awareness, black pride, black dignity. It's neither boastful nor aggressive, but it's a powerful force.

It's because of his desire to identify with something broader in scope than the Afro-West Indian that he chose an 'African' name for his daughter. He himself had no idea about how to find an African name so his scholarly team-mate Peter Roebuck came to his assistance. He thumbed through a few books in the library in Taunton and came up with the name Matara, which according to Richards means 'some kind of African princess'. Thus was his first-born named.

It's doubtful whether Richards has ever taken more than a passing interest in Rastafarianism. But he is proud of his Rasta friends. His interest in them and in their religion derives more from the fact that in some circles in England and in the West Indies, they appear to be discriminated against because of what they believe and because of their unconventional appearance.

He says:

> I went to school with a lot of these guys and they are my friends. Even in Antigua, people feel that it is not quite the thing for Viv Richards to have friends among the Rastas. One person even went as far as to say that if I wanted to go further in West Indian cricket then perhaps it would not be a good idea for me to be seen with such people. But I feel very strongly that that's prejudiced. And I am certainly not going to change my friends for anybody.
>
> I am not a believer totally in the whole philosophy of Rastafarianism, I only go as far as the fact that some of my friends have given me some of the things they believe in. But I believe that Charity begins at home and I do not like the way Rastas are

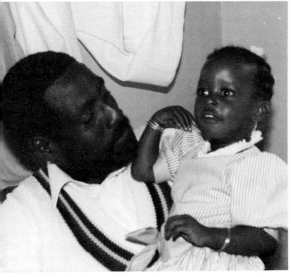

Father and daughter, Matara, in Taunton . . .

. . . and Antigua

treated in some parts of the Caribbean. We in the third world cannot afford to behave in that kind of prejudiced way. I think it's bad.

Third world people must learn to share everything with all its people and not discriminate against them simply because they are Rastas or whatever.

I know that some good prospects in West Indies cricket have not got as far as they could because they wear long hair in the Rasta style. There's one player, Scotland, a left-arm spinner. People have been murmuring that he can't play unless he looks more conventional. I don't think that's right.

All this helps to sharpen his views about ever playing cricket in South Africa, in a society where discrimination is institutionalised.

I have never been to South Africa, of course, but there are

131

Ian Botham: if he played in South Africa he could never look Viv in the face again

people whose views I respect. They are not loonies or radicals, moderate people who know what the position is in that country. You hear about changes in the South African system, but I know from what I hear that there is still a long way to go. While conditions are as they are, it's not very difficult for me to turn down all the attractive offers I get. Ian Botham, one of the hottest properties in the game, you know, he turned down an offer to play in South Africa. And he said a very nice thing. He said: 'If I go to South Africa, I could never look Viv Richards in the face again.' So, how could I go?

I don't know what the long-term position of the English 'rebels' will be. I don't know whether Gooch and Emburey will get back into the England side. But that's their affair and not too much of my concern.

I could see the day when people might play in South Africa in a more accepted way. But that place will have to make a lot of changes first. And I would have to be convinced in my own mind that the political climate had improved, that everybody was getting a fair crack, before I thought of going.

It's difficult not to come to the conclusion that some of the English and West Indian cricketers who have gone there for a lot of money are being used. I think that has now become obvious. But I still don't want to criticise what others do. Every man must make up his own mind. I have made up mine.

Richards believes that he should use his position as one of the top players in the world to draw attention to the cries of black liberation movements and to South African racism. His views about South Africa and about not playing cricket there certainly strike a chord in West Indian public opinion.

Those West Indian players who made the tour were called 'Judas cricketers' and the tour was dubbed a 'Judas tour.' Typical of the flood of letters in newspapers or magazines was this one published in the Trinidad *Express* on Friday 11 February 1983:

Above everything else, the actions of the West Indian cricketers in South Africa show them as being illiterate, greedy, unprincipled, treacherous, easily bought and lacking in foresight and understanding of world affairs.

I wonder if they know why South Africa left the Commonwealth; if they ever heard of Sharpville, Soweto, Nelson Mandela, Steve Biko, Chief Luthilu or any of their black brothers who were and are still being murdered, tortured and deprived of even the most simple freedoms and human rights.

To raise the excuse of financial hardship and want is to be dishonest and deceitful. In the same way our intellectuals could use the same argument.

What is more shameful is that some sections of the media seem to encourage deceit in advancing the views of some persons that the West Indian governments have not provided incentives to sportsmen and therefore the so-called rebel cricketers were forced to accept filthy lucre from South Africa.

I urge all governments concerned to deprive those cricketers of entry to their countries and to force them to live in South Africa as politicians, cricketers, or better still as honorary citizens.

I compliment the authorities in Antigua for detaining Parry.

I wonder if they can't be deprived of their citizenship.

I say to every decent West Indian, disown them, subjugate them, ban them, deport them.

It's a burning shame.

I hope the world does not judge all West Indians on the basis of the actions of those greedy traitors.

The crowning accolade to such sentiments was the fact that during Trinidad's carnival in 1983, the calypsonian who was judged that year's best, sung a calypso about the 'Judas cricketers'. His was a more equivocal judgment than the stern letter in the Trinidad *Express*. The final line of the song though was: 'To hell with South Africa.'

Richards can hardly ever be persuaded to discuss it at any length, but he has been quite deeply hurt by racist slurs directed against him in English cricket. While, in a charmingly naive way, he would like to entertain the belief that cricket crowds (unlike those at some football grounds in England where racist fascist groups command an entire section of the stand) should be pure and unprejudiced, he's had to contend with abusive shouts: 'You black bastard' is the first thing that comes out of some guy's mouth when the tension rises.

Richards stops short of talking too much about his reaction to such comments from the crowd, but most of his team-mates agree that people who make them would be advised to stay well hidden from the man. His anger at racist shouts could be quite fearsome.

Peter Roebuck remembers batting with Richards on one occasion when someone shouted something from the crowd. Richards glared at the offending section of the spectators and hit the next ball he received back to the bowler with such anger and force that the hapless bowler had to be carried off the field.

Richards remains acutely sensitive to the attitude of the West Indies cricket authorities. At times, he believes he still sees a yearning in Caribbean cricket officialdom for the 'old days', when players were less independent, and when their attitude to the cricket bosses amounted almost to genuflection.

Towards the end of the 1983 cricket season, Richards heard on the radio, during a Championship match against Surrey at Taunton, that the West Indies Board had asked Clive Lloyd to continue as West

Indies captain for the 1983/84 tour of India, although it had been widely assumed that Richards might replace him as captain for that tour.

Richards has said that he would regard the captaincy of the West Indies as the greatest honour of his playing career, and towards the end of the 1982 English cricket season, Lloyd, still playing like a giant, had indicated that he might stand down and pass the mantle of leadership to Viv Richards.

There was little doubt that Richards was disappointed to learn that Lloyd had been asked to carry on as captain. He suddenly became deeply suspicious of the motives of the West Indies Board in asking Clive Lloyd to contine. And he felt it might be a personal slight. But just to show how deeply West Indian players still feel about the darker pre-Frank-Worrell age of West Indian cricket, Richards' response to Lloyd's being asked to stay on was: 'They're probably looking for some blue-eyed blond boy,' he said, 'one whose hair falls in place at the shake of his head.'

It was, in its way, quite an extraordinary comment. It showed that the great gap of understanding between the West Indies Board and the West Indies players is still alarmingly wide.

An interesting footnote to the request by the West Indies authorities to Lloyd to stay on as captain was that it came on the very day that Richards learned that his 'acting' captaincy of Somerset was about to come to an end.

Rose had been kept out of the Somerset side for most of the 1983 season through injury and, with Ian Botham called up for test duty against New Zealand, Richards had been leading the county side. The club had thought that Richards may be able to continue the captaincy because of Ian Botham's international commitments. However, the night before the news of the request to Lloyd, Ian Botham, Somerset's vice-captain, had called up club president Colin Atkinson, saying that he was hoping to resume his leadership of the team in intervals when he wasn't playing for England, and later on at the end of the New Zealand tour.

Ian Botham returned to lead Somerset, and Viv Richards lost two captaincies on the same day.

CHAPTER TEN

*... the presence of Richards, the world's greatest
player, was an inspiration to the side. There
seldom seemed much reason for him not to make
a large and entertaining score and his runs came
so fast that he could be given by way of a rest,
a lower place in the order and still have time
to make a telling contribution. It would be hard
to overpraise Richards, either for the brilliance
with which he bats or the spirit in which he plays
the game*

John Woodcock
Wisden 1981

The summer of 1979 marked the beginning of a very crowded and tiring programme of cricket for Viv Richards. It took its toll on his stamina in the end: he suffered from groin strain; he had trouble with his back; and he batted in some matches in excruciating pain. To make matters worse, he thought he might have developed a serious eye infection. For a long time it seemed that only surgery would correct the condition, but fortunately his sight improved in the troublesome eye.

After his season with Somerset, Richards went on tour with the West Indies to Australia for a three-match test series and for the limited-over Benson and Hedges World Series Cup. One of the concommitants of the Packer influence was that Australian tours became longer and more strenuous.

Later that same year, the West Indies returned to England to play five test matches, and then it was off to Pakistan for another series of four tests before going home to the West Indies to prepare to play against England.

He may never have repeated the prodigious feats of his 1976 season in England, but Richards batting continued to dominate his side's performances.

OPPOSITE Joel Garner excelled with the bat and the ball in Somerset's first honour in more than a hundred years *(George Herringshaw)*

137

In the 1979 Gillette Cup final, it was Richards' innings that steered Somerset to victory. His 117 was a model of aggression and deliberate caution. He had determined to make sure that Somerset would never again come so agonisingly close to winning their first major title, only to see the opportunity slip away again. As he'd done on so many occasions in the past, he stamped his own authority on the game. His team was never in danger of losing while he remained in control out in the middle.

That first Somerset honour in 104 years was made all the sweeter by the fact that Richards and his fellow West Indian Joel Garner shared a record eighth wicket partnership nearing the end of the game. That he was still there was also an indication of how long Richards was determined to stay to make sure his side was safe. He had batted for nearly three and a half hours and was without question the man of the match. Somerset's joy knew no bounds in that summer of 1979 when they also won the John Player League.

What had been said about his contribution to the West Indies team was just as true in Somerset's case: 'The presence of the world's greatest player was an inspiration.'

The 1979 English summer had been rather inclement; Richards played only sixteen Championship matches and scored just over a thousand runs. He got 106 against Yorkshire at Harrogate, a fine hundred against Leicestershire and had a memorable knock of 156 against Middlesex at Lords.

Richards and the West Indies had a great deal to prove when they set out for Australia at the end of 1979. In five previous tours to that country, the West Indians had always been losers and four years before they'd been totally destroyed by the pace attack of Dennis Lillee and Jeff Thomson, and by their own indifferent batting and lack of discipline.

That the West Indies turned the tables on Australia to take the Worrell Trophy, and also beat England in the final of the Benson and Hedges World Series Cup was due in no small part to the imperious batting of Viv Richards. He was voted the most outstanding player of both the test and the limited-over series ... a notable

OPPOSITE Sydney 1979: being presented with the man of the series award by commentator Tony Greig ...
... and (INSET) Geoff Boycott joins in the congratulations (*both Adrian Murrell*)

138

achievement as he batted in considerable pain on several occasions.

Greg Chappell, one of the finest batsmen ever to grace the game, has said that one of the best innings he has ever seen was the one played by Viv Richards at the Adelaide Oval during that 1979/80 tour. The wicket had been helpful to the bowlers, but Richards, who believes that a good batsman should be able to score runs on any wicket, had the Australian bowlers in full retreat, scoring 76 runs before lunch to give the West Indies the initiative in the match.

His 76 in the first innings was followed by another fine knock of 74 in the second. He had begun his test series with a brilliant century against Australia at Brisbane and reached 140 before he was splendidly caught by wicket keeper, Rodney Marsh. In that test match, Rowe got 50 and Joel Garner 60, but the West Indies' 441 in the first innings owed everything to the foundation laid by Richards.

The first test ended in a draw, but the West Indies made no mistake in pressing home their advantage in the other two.

In the second test Australia elected to have first strike, and although they lost only one wicket before lunch, their innings folded quickly as they only managed a score of 156.

The West Indies began their reply with an intimidating attack on the Australian quickies. Richards' 50 came in even time after he'd been particularly vicious to Rodney Hogg, hitting him for a lofty six to the furthest corner of the Melbourne Cricket ground, and continuing with audacious skill to strike several fours all round the wicket. He was out for 96, the West Indies made 397.

Australia's second turn at the crease produced only a marginally better total than their first innings score and the West Indies coasted to victory by ten wickets. Richards was named man of the match. That was beginning to happen with almost embarrassing regularity!

The West Indies won the third test by a massive 408 runs and Richards was again named man of the match for his consistently brilliant batting in both innings. His average for that Australian test tour was an incredible 98.66 in all first-class matches. His test-match average was 96.50, outstripping by far all the other West Indian

OPPOSITE The batting of Viv Richards helped the West Indies to win the Worrell Trophy for the first time *(Adrian Murrell)*

LEFT OVERLEAF Richards getting the better of the scurge of the West Indies batting, Dennis Lillee, in the Brisbane test 1979 *(Adrian Murrell)*
RIGHT Hooking Lillee – one-day match Melbourne 1979 *(Adrian Murrell)*

batsmen. In the Benson and Hedges World Cup series his runs were: 9, 153 not out, 62, 85 not out, 88, 23 and 65.

Australians are unlikely to ever forget the West Indies match against Australia in Melbourne on 9 December. Twelve days before, Australia had beaten the West Indies by five wickets in Sydney. Richards failed to get into double figures in that game and his problems with his back continued on into the second meeting between the two teams. He was given a pain-killing injection just before he went out to bat and, hobbling noticeably throughout his innings, he took the Australian attack apart. His 153 runs came after 131 balls. He'd struck one six and 16 fours. It had become virtually impossible to plug the gaps he found in the field.

The West Indies scorecard shows the extent to which there had always been only one player in the match:

Greenidge c Marsh b Lillee 11,
Haynes c Marsh b Thomson 80,
Richards not out 153,
Kallicharan not out 16.

And so the West Indies came to England for five test matches and two Prudential Trophy limited-over games.

The West Indies took the series by virtue of having beaten England in the Trent Bridge test, but they were easily the better team, and their batting was again dominated by Richards. He topped the first-class and the test-match averages and began something of a controversy for his unforgettable assault on the England fast bowler, Bob Willis.

Newspaper reports at the time claimed it was a vendetta, but Richards denied that this was the case. Talking to him now, however, three years after his savage attack on Willis' bowling, it emerges that he's always been waiting for the opportunity to have a punishing go at Willis. He'd kept at the back of his mind a rather unfriendly encounter with Willis in the West Indies. Richards had been a young hopeful then, still struggling to impress the Antiguan cricket authorities and to force his way into the West Indian side. In his own words, Willis had given him 'a hard time'. He sent down a few bouncers, three or four whistled past his head, and eventually had Richards trapped in the deep, trying the hook shot. Richards vowed to avenge this, and when during the 1980 tour Willis talked about having 'a plan' to get his wicket, Richards decided the time had come to teach the England fast bowler a lesson.

His opportunity came in the fourth test against England at Manchester. The depressing weather weighed rather heavily on the game and England's first innings did nothing to lift the gloom. They were all out for 150, having been put in to bat by Clive Lloyd. The West Indies began equally badly, losing Greenidge without scoring and Haynes for 1. But the plight of the West Indies went almost unnoticed as Richards turned on Willis with singular malevolence. He took 53 of his 63 runs off Willis, hitting the England bowler back over his head, driving him powerfully through the covers and hoisting anything short over the ropes on the onside for four. It was a brutal display of unrestrained batting skill and Willis was powerless to do anything about it. England's and Willis' agony ended when, to his delight, Richards' Somerset team-mate, Ian Botham, bowled him between bat and pad.

In the second test at Lords Richards, who had missed the corresponding fixture four years earlier, helped the West Indies to a score of 518 with a dazzling innings of 145. He was again voted man of the match. One hundred of his runs came in boundaries, and they included one six. His innings ended when he gave an easy catch to square-leg.

Towards the end of the tour, in a three-day fixture against Warwickshire, Richards' score of 41 in his team's second innings came in spectacular fashion. It included three sixes and five fours. He was terribly harsh on Clifford, whom he hit in seven consecutive balls for: 4–6–6–4–4–6–4.

He scored five centuries that summer playing for the West Indies:

> 145 against England at Lords,
> 131 against Northants at Milton Keynes,
> 122 against Essex at Chelmsford,
> 103 against Somerset at Taunton, and
> 100 against Glamorgan at Swansea.

And to think the poor England players were about to see more of Richards' broad bat later that same year on his home ground in the West Indies.

The remainder of the summer left him little time to make up for his absence from Somerset. But at Bristol he hammered the Gloucestershire bowlers for 170, before he set off for the West Indies.

Many English counties were beginning to develop the line of thought that since it was virtually impossible not to be out-gunned by the 'in form' Richards if he was attacked, containment was the best policy. That meant trying to bowl defensively at him. But Viv Richards believes, as Percy Fender wrote in *The Game of Cricket*: 'Defensive tactics in bowling never include the type which permits the batsmen to rest inactive ball after ball.'

Richards knows that there is hardly ever in a game of cricket a point of equilibrium between bat and ball, bowler and batsman. One or the other invariably gets the upper hand. Richards' aim is to make sure he does.

He is sufficiently confident and skilful to blast to smithereens the best-laid defensive strategies of any team.

The Guyana test match was cancelled when the authorities decided that because of his 'South African connections', Robin Jackman, a member of the England party, was not welcome in Guyana. England did the only possible thing in the circumstances and the whole team left Georgetown.

The incident was a sharp reminder of how bitterly opposed some West Indian governments are to South Africa's apartheid, and the lengths to which they are prepared to go to demonstrate that disapproval. From a cricket point of view, the England tour administrators felt they could not appear to comply with a policy which amounted to the exercise of a veto on who may or may not represent England. That remains the best argument. West Indian governments are unmoved by hysterical press strictures about political interference in sport.

The visit by England to the West Indies was also marred by the death of Ken Barrington, England's tour manager.

Against this unhappy background, Richards had a great deal to remember about the 1980/81 England tour. He married his childhood sweetheart, Miriam, (the entire ceremony was broadcast on national radio) and he was again the sheet anchor of his team's batting.

He also reversed his run of poor performances in test matches in Barbados when he scored a century there in the third test. England faced a highly disciplined and determined Richards on that tour. He

OPPOSITE 1981 was a year to remember. Marriage to his childhood sweetheart, Miriam

146

cut loose when he found the deliveries to hit and lost none of his audacious stroke play, but he also demonstrated he had the patience to build an innings. For long periods in that Barbados test match he was uncharacteristically quiet, but he always seemed to be able to quicken the pace at will and force his opponents onto the defensive. His 182 in Barbados was excellent preparation for the fourth test match in St John's.

There could not possibly have been a happier combination of events for Richards: he was playing for the West Indies a few days after his wedding and doing so in Antigua, where a test match was being played for the first time. He was playing before his country-men, who had put his face on national stamps and dubbed him Antigua's ambassador.

The night before the West Indies batted in that test match, all Antigua speculated and willed their native son to grace the historic occasion with a fine performance. It is a measure of the esteem in which Richards holds his countrymen that he was perhaps more nervous going out to bat in that test match than he'd ever been before. The ground was tense, a capacity crowd urging their hero to do well. It seemed such a short time since he had first played club cricket and represented the Leeward Islands there.

Ridding himself of his tension, Richards began his innings in explosive mood. His first 50 came almost entirely in boundaries. With every one, the very foundations of Antigua seem to tremble with acclamation. His forcing shots off the back foot were a delight to watch and he square drove the England slow and medium-pace bowlers with effortless ease.

After his tremendous start, Richards went into his shell for a time, intent on ensuring that he got a big score. His century when it came was by no means his best, nor did it approach the brilliance of some of the knocks he'd played in other parts of the world. But to this day, it would be impossible to get anyone in Antigua to believe that.

'Vivi' had done what was required. His career had come full circle. It was as if with that century his cricket had achieved its sense of fulfilment. Swollen with pride, all Antigua joined in the celebration.

His average on the tour was 85. He had scored 340 runs in the tests.

1981 was a glorious year for Richards and for Somerset.

For the first time in its history, Somerset won the Benson and

Hedges Cup. Richards' contribution was a beautifully paced innings and a score of 132 not out in the final against Surrey at Lords. There was never any doubting who would be nominated man of the match.

Somerset were second in the John Player League and third in the County Championship. It had been another great season for a club breaking into the big time mainly because of the consistently great match-winning performances of Richards, Botham and Garner.

The season was studded with dazzling displays of batting by Richards. On a difficult wicket at Weston-super-Mare, he battled his way to 150. At Bath in June he'd scored his first hundred of the season against Nottinghamshire, hitting two sixes and thirteen fours. It was the first of nine hundreds scored that year, 2,500 runs in all.

His phenomenal contribution to the success of his club becomes all too apparent when his centuries are listed:

106 against Nottinghamshire at Bath,
118 against Worcestershire at Worcester,
196 against Leicestershire at Leicester,
130 against Derby at Taunton,
153 against Yorkshire at Sheffield,
150 against Worcestershire at Weston-super-Mare,
128 against Sussex at Taunton.

Richards was awarded a benefit by Somerset in 1982. The chairman of the county's cricket subcommittee spoke for all Somerset supporters when, in asking for their support, he wrote: 'We have been fortunate indeed to have him, not only for his influence on the field, but as an ambassador off it. No one can truly estimate the value of his presence to our club.' That value to Somerset continued in 1982 and 1983.

During the 1982 season a nagging finger injury troubled him for long periods, but he still scored more first-class runs than any other player in the Somerset side.

He scored his first hundred of the season against Kent in early May (146 in fifty-five overs) and it was not until the end of the season that he again demonstrated his true mastery by scoring 178 out of Somerset's total of 307 against Lancashire.

Like so many other professional cricketers, Richards has showed signs of the strain involved in playing cricket virtually twelve months of the year. He is occasionally out to lazy shots. At other times his concentration, which can be so obviously intense, is lost. Fortu-

nately, even when he is not in his best form, he can still summon up the strength and the determination to take an attack apart and swing the game in his team's favour.

Before his benefit year, there'd been Benson and Hedges World Cup cricket in Australia, a long tiring schedule of matches, made especially so if your team was successful. Richards was out without scoring once, but only on four occasions did he fail to reach double figures and his other scores of 47, 72, 32, 41, 36, 64, 78, 60 and 70 were solid, workmanlike contributions to the West Indies' second victory in the competition.

Despite his batting and his leadership, the Leeward Islands have remained near the bottom of the Shell Shield competition in the West Indies. But at the end of the 1981/82 season Richards scored a majestic 167 in front of his home crowd at the Antigua Recreation Ground. Playing cricket in Antigua is always a great thrill for Richards. His preparation and training schedules are as rigorous as they are before playing for Somerset or the West Indies. He expresses his gratitude to Antigua by never giving anything less than his best.

Cricket in 1983 began for Viv Richards in the West Indies. And the season started on the note of controversy over the decision of a few leading players to go to South Africa as 'honorary whites' to play for large sums of money.

But by mid-February the focus had shifted to the visit of the Indian cricket team, led by allrounder Kapil Dev.

Richards spent the early part of the season travelling between Antigua and Barbados seeing specialists about an injury to his hand. Just before the first test on 23 February at Sabina Park in Jamaica, he was passed fit.

The West Indies won the toss and put their opponents in to bat. Clive Lloyd sent his fast bowlers into battle and by tea India were 127 for 7 and appeared totally at sea. But Sharma and Sandhu helped the score past 200 and India reached the height of respectability with a final score of 251.

When they batted the West Indies were pinned down for long periods by an accurate Indian spin attack. Greenidge was made to toil with great patience and application for his 70, but none of the other West Indian batsmen really mastered the guiles of Shastri and

OPPOSITE The face of determined aggression: batting for the West Indies in 1983 (ASP)

Venkataraghavan. Richards never looked very happy against the turning ball and was out for 29. He remembers the delivery from Shastri which accounted for his wicket: 'It was a well-flighted ball, pitched well and spun away. I didn't middle the shot and was easily caught.'

The West Indies captain Clive Lloyd made 24 and Dujon 29 before the West Indies innings ended on 254, a lead of 3 runs on India's first innings score.

India's start when they batted a second time couldn't have been more inauspicious. Gasvaskar went first ball, bowled through the gate by Holding, and although Armarnath and Gaekwad put on more than 50 for the second wicket to steady the innings, India had slumped to 81 for 3 by close of play. The match seemed destined for a quiet draw when rain washed out the fourth day's play and delayed the start of the final day's. That prediction seemed confirmed when by tea on that last day, with the West Indies still to have their second turn at the crease, India were 167 for 6.

Then came an unforgettable dramatic spell of fast bowling by Andy Roberts. He picked up the wicket of Kirmani after tea, first ball, had Sandhu caught in the gully off the fifth and got the wicket of Venkat off the last ball of the over. Suddenly, the West Indies saw a chink of light and the outside possibility of trying to force a win. In just over half an hour and 20 overs, they were asked to score 172 runs. Greenidge and Haynes led the assault against Kapil Dev and they put on 46 before the first wicket went. When the second wicket fell a mere 19 runs later, it looked as though the West Indies would fail to get the required runs. The asking rate was 6.6 runs per over.

But Richards came to the rescue. Off 36 deliveries he slammed his way to 61 magnificent runs, including four sixes and five fours, and when he was out attempting to hit Armanath out of the ground his side needed only sixteen more runs with two overs remaining. The West Indies made it; Dujon lifting Armanath for a giant six, amid scenes of incredible excitement.

Having won that first match, when it looked as though it was going to end in a tame draw, we really felt on top of the world. It's just the sort of start you need. The boys felt good, the crowds were with us and I had managed to play quite well,

OPPOSITE Against India in the World Cup 1983 . . . before the rot set in *(Adrian Murrell)*

152

putting the pressure on the Indian side just when we needed to. But the second test was bleak for me, although I got among the runs again in Guyana.

Richards made 109 in that third test in Guyana, but the game was ruined by rain and ended in a draw. He got 80 in the fourth test, helping his side to victory by ten wickets, and ended with a modest aggregate of 282 runs in the series for an average of 47.

Richards left the West Indies for England and for the summer of 1983, hardly realising that he was to see a great deal more of the Indian team than the West Indies had bargained for. Conventional wisdom held that the West Indies were by far the best one-day, limited-over-game teams in the world and it was in that spirit that Clive Lloyd and his team approached the 1983 Prudential World Cup.

Looking back at it now, although the West Indian cricketers are still reluctant to admit it, hubris had set in. The West Indies rather arrogantly felt that having won it twice before, the World Cup had become theirs by divine right.

The 'gods' usually sound a warning of a cruel fate to come, and had the West Indies players been that inclined they might have read the signs. The first engagement in the Prudential series was against India and they were defeated by a comfortable margin of 34 runs.

India, batting first at Old Trafford, reached 262 for 8 off their allotted sixty overs, a respectable total built mainly around a fine knock of 89 by Yashpal Sharma. No West Indian batsman stayed long enough to dictate the terms of the game, Richards was caught behind for 17, Greenidge and Haynes got 24 runs apiece and the ever-reliable skipper chipped in with 25. But it was left to Andy Roberts and Joel Garner to put the Indians on the defensive for the first time in the match. By that time the West Indies needed 84 runs, with almost all of their batting gone and with only twelve overs to get them.

When Joel Garner ventured down the pitch to drive once too often and was beaten by the turning ball, the West Indies were still a long way from India's first-innings tally, and Kapil Dev and his players jumped and hugged themselves with joy.

When the West Indies swept by Australia at Headingley a few days later to win by the convincing margin of 101 runs, it looked as though they had put behind them the nightmare of India's victory at

Old Trafford. Richards didn't get into double figures against the Australians but the team performance had been a thoroughly competent one.

One week after their defeat at Old Trafford, the West Indies got their own back on Kapil Dev's side. And the hero of the West Indian innings was Viv Richards. Fighting to regain his form, he seemed to judge each stroke with extravagant care, putting on 80 runs with his captain and staying at his post until the fifty-second over, by which time he had scored a workmanlike hundred. In their reply India never recovered from losing their opening pair with only 21 runs on the board and fell well short of the West Indies score of 282.

Three days later, Richards made 95 not out as the West Indies again beat Australia, this time by 7 wickets.

On 22 June the West Indies met Pakistan in the semi-final of the Prudential World Cup at the Oval. The ground was filled to capacity. Pakistan's middle order collapsed in a pitiable bundle and at the conclusion of their allotted 60 overs they had scored only 184 runs. The West Indies lost Greenidge and Haynes in the gentle chase, but Richards' 80 not out, hitting the ball fiercely to all parts of the field, and Gomes' 50 not out saw the West Indies safely home.

For a long time, during the course of Pakistan's innings, which never seemed destined for great things, the buzz around the Oval had been of the prospect of an England v. West Indies final. England were playing India at Manchester on the same day.

But the England captain Bob Willis decided to bat first and his team was restricted to 213 runs by some steady, accurate Indian bowling.

When India were two down with only 50 runs on the board, it looked as though they would struggle for the runs. But Armanath, Sharma and Patil played sensibly, the England attack was blunted and India had reached a World Cup final for the first time.

The final of a Cricket World Cup competition generates an electricity and an atmosphere of its own and the 1983 tournament was no different. When the West Indies arrived at the ground it was already comfortably full, and the prospect of another World Cup victory must have been very sweet to the senses. The West Indies won the toss, Lloyd invited Kapil Dev to have first strike and when Gavaskar was snapped up behind off Roberts for two, there was a feeling that the old old story of West Indies supremacy in one-day cricket was about to assert itself. With more than half their overs

In the World Cup final at Lords
Kapil Dev takes command

(Adrian Murrell)

Not quite! India took the trophy in 1983 for the first time ever (*ASP*)

gone, India were 92 for the loss of the top half of their batting line-up, and not a man could be found who would bet against a West Indies victory. India reached an unimpressive score of 183 before they were all out.

The West Indies began badly, but no one paid any notice: they have frequently done so in the past, only to steady themselves and produce the maturity in batting later on in an innings to get the required runs.

Richards, batting at number three, certainly showed no concern about the quality of the Indian attack. He hit Madan Lal for three fours in his first over and the only question seemed when the West Indies would overhaul India's score. But Haynes fell, giving an easy catch at cover for apparently no reason at all, and then Lloyd pulled a muscle and was forced to ask for a runner, and then came the real body blow to the West Indies.

Richards seemed to get into position quickly to swing Madan Lal high and handsomely over mid-wicket, but the Indian captain Kapil Dev, running back, never lost sight of the ball, and just managing to get his hands to it, he held a magnificent catch. Richards had been on 33 then and no other batsman was to approach that personal contribution. Dujon got 25, Marshall made a brave 18, but from 76 for 5 the West Indies folded tamely and almost without a whimper for 140.

The explosion of Indian joy at Lords on that memorable day and its echoes thousands of miles away in the streets of Delhi and Bombay were to become part of a cricket legend.

The sounds were to haunt the West Indies team throughout the night and for many months later. It's what many players remember, much more so than they do details of the game. Richards himself can offer no convincing explanation for what happened, although he maintains it taught the West Indies players a lesson about the way other countries reward their players for World Cup success.

I thought I was going quite well until I miscued one from Madan Lal and Kapil Dev took a good catch. It was a very good catch.

'For the rest, we just lost a match. When you win all the time, it's expected of you and people are surprised when you don't.

The most painful thing for us was to hear those Indian drums around our hotel all night. Some of the guys broke down. Marshall, who had played so well during the whole tournament took it particularly badly. He cried. I can only remember not being able to get through the hotel lobby for celebrating Indian supporters.

What is really annoying is to hear that some West Indians at home thought we had thrown the match or something like that. That really hurts. If you don't win all the time, our public has no time for you, man.

And to learn how the Indian people made heroes of their players when they got home makes you think. Do you know, some of the players got flats in Delhi as part of their prize for winning the World Cup? We won two World Cups and got to the final of the third and we have no luxury flats. All we got was a little cash and World Cup medals. No flats though. I think it taught us a great lesson all that.'

Richards had not been at his dominating best during the World Cup, but he was consistently among the honours. In rounds four and five and in the semi-finals, he won man of the match awards, more than any other player in the entire competition.

And when three months later he went back to Lords with Somerset to play Kent in the Nat West Bank Trophy Final, his half-century, the top score for Somerset that day, made it certain that Kent and not Somerset would be the losers that time.

That season for Somerset, he played 12 matches, 20 innings, scored 5 hundreds and made altogether 1204 runs. He topped the first class batting averages, yet again.

Despite his continuing success in scoring runs, Richards can hardly ever be tempted to join in any discussion about whether he is as good a player as Hammond or Bradman. Sometimes he's found it impossible to prevent comparisons being forced on him. In the summer of 1977 he was awarded £500 for hitting the highest number of sixes (73) in that year. The record had previously been held by Arthur Wellard, another great cricket name from the past.

He says:

I can't say whether I am as good a player as whoever people care to bring up. My job is to play to the best of my ability and to make runs as best as I can. It's impossible to compare with players of old days. You don't know what kind of conditions they played under, whether the bowling was as tight or whether the field placing was as keen. I think these comparisons are a waste of time, if even they are very flattering to me. I don't think about it much. I'm just out there to do what I'm in the side to do – to make runs.

He believes that the technical efficiency required to play the game at the highest level has probably never changed that much, and that in any event the really good player will always be able to tailor his batting to the circumstances. That's why he remains so unconcerned about discussions of good or bad wickets and about field placings designed to restrict his scoring opportunities. He believes that the job of a batsman, if it's done well, is to find a method to overcome such problems. He says repeatedly that it's his job to score runs and that if he fails he's not doing his job. What the other players on the park are up to is of very little concern to him.

Richards prides himself on being the complete cricketer. His reflexes in close fielding positions are superb. He moves with lightning speed in the outfield and his mere presence near the ball, however well-struck, is a deterrent to any batsman trying to steal an extra run.

He is very modest about his bowling and will talk more readily

about the times he's been carted around the field than the occasions when, at crucial stages of limited-over matches, he's bowled his off-breaks well enough to keep the runs in check. In the 1983 season he also claimed six wickets in an innings. Regardless of what he says, though, like most batsmen, he loves to bowl.

And his bowling has got better. He can turn the ball a long way on helpful wickets; he bowls a straighter one; and batsmen tempted to lift him over the infield always run the risk of being caught in the deep.

At a vital point in the Benson and Hedges World Cup Series in Australia, the West Indies defeated Pakistan by the slim margin of 18 runs, partly because the Pakistani batsmen were pinned down for a long time by the accurate bowling of Richards and were thus unable to give their innings the acceleration it needed near the end. Richards' ten overs cost him only 52 runs, not untidy for a limited-over match and with a team trying to increase the tempo of an innings.

It was perhaps as a result of that incident that the Pakistan batsmen resolved never again to be kept quiet by Richards' slow off-breaks. When the two teams met again the Pakistanis decided to throw caution to the winds when facing Richards, and they paid the penalty. He claimed the prized scalps of Zaheer Abass, Javed Miandad and Wasin Raja. Any front-line bowler in the world would be proud of such a haul. Richards had destroyed Pakistan's middle-order batting.

In June during the 1982 County Championship season, he sent down 13 overs for only 26 runs and in the process picked up the wickets of three Gloucestershire batsmen, Stovold, Broad and Bainbridge.

So that in a season when his batting never reached the heady heights of former years, he was still able to play an important role in Somerset's effort. Richards believes that this allround ability is important. He is so aware of what he must live up to, even when he is not scoring as many runs as everyone has come to expect of him. One year after he joined Somerset Eric Hill wrote: 'Richards, a wonderful phenomenon, made the biggest impact of any Somerset player since Gimblett in 1935.'

It goes without saying that he would very much like the job of leading the West Indies as captain. He has deputised for Clive Lloyd,

OPPOSITE On the way to topping the County Championship first-class batting averages yet again in 1983 (ASP)

a player and captain for whom his admiration is unbounded, and he has led Somerset when he's been called upon to do so. He is a thoughtful captain; he reads the game well, and he demonstrates a shrewd appreciation of strategy and has always been good at motivating his team.

There are endless stories from Somerset players of Viv Richards willing his team-mates to match-winning performances by dressing-room pep talks.

When he deputised for Ian Botham during the 1983 season, he put himself lower down in the batting order to give an opportunity to some of the younger Somerset players to establish themselves by settling down to playing long innings.

It was also an attempt on Richards' part to relieve himself of the enormous pressure which comes with the knowledge that so frequently Somerset's fortunes hang on whether or not he gets a big score.

OPPOSITE Like most batsmen, Richards loves to bowl (*Adrian Murrell*)

CHAPTER ELEVEN

We touch reality most deeply, where men
struggle, fail and triumph

Anon

The West Indies went to India towards the end of 1983 with the memory of their defeat in the Prudential World Cup still fresh in their minds and still burnt on the team's soul.

Commentators in countries that had never won the World Cup had remarked with lofty detachment how good it was for cricket that such an unexpected result came at the climax of so ambitious a cricket tournament. The speculation about the good it would do to Indian cricket was endless.

None of this assuaged hurt West Indian feelings. India's victory had shaken the team's self-confidence to its roots, and although it is not in the nature of contemporary players to haunt themselves in reliving painful memories, during the 1983 Indian tour players, unasked, returned time and again to the World Cup.

It would have been unthinkable for any one player to accept responsibility for the West Indies defeat. Nevertheless, it had been taken for granted that had Viv Richards stayed the team might have had a chance of getting closer to the Indian score. When his wicket fell the BBC television commentator had called it the turning-point in the game, and India's jubilation on the field told the crowd at Lords that the rank outsiders felt they were on the way to a historic victory. It's the kind of pressure with which Viv Richards has had to cope as the team's number one batsman.

Of course, had I batted a little longer,' he says, 'the course of the game could have been different. But that could apply to other batsmen as well. Cricket is a team game. And anyhow, you can't play back these games and wonder what might have happened . . . if. You just have to try to do better next time. My business is scoring runs and I didn't get as many as I would have liked in that game. That's pretty obvious.

In India the West Indians found a new channel for expressing the pain of defeat. Everywhere they went there were reminders of the nationwide party that had been held to celebrate India's World Cup success. One block away from the team's hotel in Bombay there were still banners strung across busy main streets, proclaiming the mastery of Sunil Gavaskar and Kapil Dev. On brightly painted hoardings even in the dingiest parts of the city, India's World Cup victory had been adopted as the new progressive metaphor by soft-drink firms, building companies, newspapers, banks and airlines.

West Indian players saw these advertising signs every time they went to and from the Wankhede Stadium. And on almost every journey it revived the sore point among the players about the material benefits which had gone to the Indian players for winning the World Cup. Richards never managed to stop himself repeating the details of everything the Indian players had received for the World Cup victory, or from reflecting ruefully that even if the West Indies had won the rewards in the West Indies would never have been as great as they had been in India.

But the reminders of India's success had one important effect: it made the West Indies more determined than ever to avenge the defeat which had stung them so badly.

And that made the manager's job of motivating the players much easier as Wes Hall admitted: 'The worst thing India ever did was to beat the West Indies. Now the guys are so keen to get stuck into Kapil Dev and his team. The whole team seems to feel that India must be made to pay for their World Cup victory. And we intend to make them pay heavily.'

And pay heavily India did.

By the time India were beaten in the second one-day international in Baroda, the World Cup had already begun to fade far away in the minds of Indian supporters. And a former Indian captain, D. K. Gaekwad, was moved to write: 'I don't know how long the happy memories of winning the World Cup will remain if we keep losing so regularly to the West Indies in these one-day internationals.'

Gaekwad's worst fears were confirmed. By mid-December India had been mauled in every single one of the five limited-over internationals. Asked to overhaul a modest Indian total of 178 for seven off the allotted 44 overs, the West Indies reached their target with 14 balls to spare and for the loss of only four wickets.

Richards did not achieve a great deal with the bat in that final

165

one-day fixture, but his bowling was effective. Having lost three wickets for 67 runs and with just about half their overs gone, the Indian batsmen were pinned down by the off-spin of Viv Richards and Roger Harper. In attempting to fight their way out of this tight corner, Armanath and Binny both fell to Richards, precipitating the final Indian collapse. Richards eight overs were bowled at the cost of only 33 runs.

India's success against the West Indies in England had been forgotten. And for the West Indian visitors so quietly indignant about how well the Indian players fared materially after the victory, there was perhaps the final consolation of the Indian captain's observation that in the one-day games his players had played terribly poorly, because the seemed for the most part to be concerned 'more with making money than playing the game seriously'.

To cause such dissension in the Indian camp was far more than the West Indies had hoped for. Their ambition had been more modest: Viv Richards confirms that in India in 1983 the West Indies were keen to regain what they felt was their rightful position as the best one-day team in the world.

> Well, not only in the one-day matches, [he says] but I think the way the fellas were very down losing at Lords. You know, in that World Cup final we just never got going. It was not one of our usual performances. It was a strange match, almost in a low key. Now, we were lucky in a way to have to play India again so soon after so we could put things right. So we could correct what we felt went wrong. I know there is nothing like luck in big cricket and, without taking away anything from India's performance in the World Cup, we are a better team. It's good to have a chance to prove it.

In the first test match at Kanpur on 21, 22, 23 and 25 October the West Indies set about proving themselves against India with a vengeance.

The West Indies batted first and India's opening attack got off to a confident start when Desmond Haynes was caught off the bowling of Kapil Dev before the score had reached double figures. Richards appeared at number three and immediately looked as though he would take the Indian bowling apart. He hit two thunderous drives off Kapil Dev and square cut Binny with fearsome power to the boundary. But just when he looked menacing, the great man fell to a ball from Kapil Dev which did just enough off the wicket to find the edge of his bat on its way through to wicket-keeper Kirmani.

The West Indies had barely a hundred runs on the board when Richards departed for 24. Trinidadian Augustine Logie was adjudged leg-before to Bhat for a duck and less than an hour later the West Indies score had sunk to 157 for 5. India's chances of containing the powerful batting line-up looked ominously good. But Gordon Greenidge took this as his cue to play one of the finest innings of his career. He was at the wicket for a shade over nine hours. Playing superbly, he took charge of a West Indian recovery with elegance and authority. Helped by Dujon, who scored a classy 81, and by Malcolm Marshall, who failed by only eight runs to reach his first-ever hundred in test cricket, Greenidge paced himself to a career best of 194. On the way, he became the twelfth West Indian batsman to reach 3,000 runs in test cricket, (after Sobers, Kanhai, Lloyd, Weekes, Fredericks, Kallicharan, Worrell, Walcott, Richards, Hunte and Butcher) and put on 130 runs for the seventh wicket with Marshall shattering the previous West Indies best (127) established by Sobers and Mendonca in Kingston, Jamaica, in 1971.

With Greenidge in command, from 157 for 5 the West Indies went on to make 454. Marshall, who had been so unrestrained in his attack on the Indian bowlers, took the new ball with Michael Holding and turned his attention to the Indian batsmen. Gavaskar was first to go. He failed to get right behind a ball which left him off the pitch and was comfortably taken behind by Dujon.

Armanath hopelessly misread another Marshall delivery which cut back into him, and went leg-before without offering a stroke. When Gaekwad edged Marshall to Dujon as Gavaskar had done before him only moments earlier, India were three wickets down with only 19 runs on their score sheet and reaching 454 suddenly looked a mountainous task.

The Indian innings went into stygian gloom when Marshall bowled Vengsrakar with an absolute beauty, and although the lower order batsmen, Madan Lal with 63 and Binny with 39, tried to restore some sanity to India's batting, their efforts had come much too late to make any appreciable difference. India scuttled out for 207 and were made to follow on. Their attempts to tame the West Indian

OVERLEAF Avenging the World Cup defeat: routing the Indians. Richards celebrates with wicket keeper Geoffrey Dujon (*Adrian Murrell*)

167

pace bowlers second time around were even more disastrous than in the first innings. The top half of the batting fell to the West Indies quick bowlers before India had scored 50, and the innings crumbled for a total of 164, giving the West Indies victory by an innings and 83 runs.

It had been Marshall's match. He had stayed with Gordon Greenidge towards the end of the West Indies innings and his bowling figures for the match were: 32 overs, 14 maidens, 66 runs, 8 wickets. Holding with 6 wickets and Davis with 5 completed India's destruction. The West Indies were ecstatic.

Richards says:

It was a wonderful way to start the test series. Gordon (Greenidge) played one of his best innings and held things together when our batting seemed in a bit of trouble early in the innings. Marshall got his highest test score and then ripped India's batting apart. He had bowled well in the World Cup, but I've never seen him faster and more controlled. It was a magnificent performance.

The second test in Delhi ended in a draw, but was marked by a controversial decision involving Viv Richards. He had been struggling to find his form and felt he was well on the way to a respectable score as he got into the sixties in the first innings. He had scored 67 when he was struck on the pad and a loud appeal went up from Kapil Dev. To his consternation, Richards looked down the track to see the umpire lift his finger. The batsman felt without doubt that he had been well outside the line of the stumps when he was struck on the pad. The umpire evidently thought otherwise and Richards was on his way back to the pavilion.

A Delhi sports magazine had this to say about Richards' dismissal and about what happened afterwards:

Was the ball doing too much in the air to suggest that the benefit of the doubt should be given to the batsman? Wasn't Viv Richards at least five feet from the wicket when he was rapped on the pads? These were the questions to ponder as the umpire held his finger up quickly on Kapil Dev's appeal for leg-before against Richards. To say the batsman was unhappy would be an understatement. A cynical smile spread across his face as he walked from the middle. There was no sign of dissent on the field, but Richards gave way to his real feelings in the dressing-room. The cups and saucers took a knock from the jumbo bat flung in anger. There was some other damage and an apology.

That was probably the most restrained of the reports of Richards' anger at what he felt was a most unfair dismissal. Much more unfortunate was the fact that the batsman's anti-Indian tirade was overheard by a number of people unconnected with cricket but very influential in political circles in Delhi. One such person was a politician described as being close to Mrs Ghandi, the Indian Prime Minister. He was not worried about the batsman's anger, but about his 'anti-Indian sentiments', which had been very loudly expressed. The view of some people in the West Indian touring party was that had Richards been captain of the West Indies, the remaining part of the Indian tour might have been in jeopardy. The matter was diplomatically dealt with by the West Indies team manager and captain, but it cast a shadow on the early part of the tour and left unanswered a number of questions about whether Richards' temperament might not occasionally let him down when he leads the West Indies.

His anger had been fuelled by his failure to get a big score in the early part of the tour – but seemed a poor excuse in the circumstances.

After the controversy of Delhi, Viv Richards did no better with the bat in the third test match at Ahmadabad. The wicket and the standard of umpiring were to be the talking-points there.

After the match the Indian commentators were convinced that everything started to go wrong for their team when the captain, Kapil Dev, decided to let the West Indies have first strike on a track which he clearly felt would give his bowlers a great deal of asssistance early on. If that was his view, then he must have also reckoned that facing the West Indies quick bowlers on a helpful wicket might have put India in considerable difficulty. All the arguments during and after the game, though, quickly became academic.

India did well to restrict their opponents to 281 runs in their first innings. The first three wickets had fallen by the time they reached 37, neither Greenidge, Haynes nor Richards reaching double figures. After that there followed a string of controversial umpiring decisions. First, Larry Gomes who had played a disciplined innings and who, in partnership with his captain Lloyd, tried to steer the West Indies to safety, was adjudged caught at slip, although his bat apparently never went near the ball. Logie, who was to bag an unenviable 'pair' in the match, was given out caught behind, although he swore he missed an attempted cut.

That meant that no other saviours were left to the West Indies but Lloyd and Dujon. Both played magnificently. The durable Clive Lloyd overcame all the problems thrown at him by the wicket and by the Indian bowlers to make a splendid 68. Dujon, who batted with the ease and distinction of a player far beyond his maturity, was most unfortunate to be out, caught off Kapil Dev, two runs short of his century.

India began their reply in confident style. Gavaskar's 90 and Gaek-wad's 39 put on 127 before they were separated. But there the glories of Indian batting ended abruptly. Kapil Dev got 31, but no other score of consequence came to India's aid. Wayne Daniel took five wickets for 39 runs in only eleven point five overs and the West Indies took a lead of 40 runs on first innings.

By the time the West Indies batted a second time, the Ahmadabad pitch was making batting more than awkward. Greenidge and Haynes were back in the pavillion before the West Indies' score reached double figures and Richards, still desperately fighting to find his touch, struggled for an hour before he was bowled by Kapil Dev for 20. Kapil Dev seemed to cause panic in the West Indies camp, although Lloyd with 33 and Gomes with 25, managed to keep him at bay, before they both succumbed. The Indian captain's remarkable figures were 30 overs, 6 maidens, 9 wickets for 83 runs.

That devastating spell bundled out the West Indies for 201, giving Lloyd and his team an overall advantage of 241 runs.

From Michael Holding's first over, India never stood a chance of getting anywhere near that total. Only three of India's batsmen reached double figures. Gavaskar was trapped leg-before for one. Five runs later Sidhu was caught behind off Holding, and after that Patil, Shastri, Binny and Kapil Dev were all out having barely opened their accounts. Holding and Davis collected seven of the wickets to tumble in the rout; Marshall picked up a couple; and India had been humiliated by 138 runs, a margin which no one would have predicted in such a low scoring match.

Controversy about the Ahmadabad wicket and about the standard of umpiring in the game continued for a long time after that West Indies victory. Viv Richards restricted his comments about both to repeating the views of the West Indies captain and of the team manager Wes Hall:

As the manager said, we began to realise just how strange everything was when a few of the Indian players came up to us and
apologised for one of our players being given out. The wicket
had been under-prepared and Kapil Dev made a major error in
giving us first strike. Our quick bowlers bowled well and Kapil
Dev's spell of 8 for 83 was a great feat, but the wicket had a great
deal to answer for. I found it a bit of a struggle, you know. The
ball was getting up sharply off a good length and the spinners
were getting bounce and turn too. But the umpiring was the
thing that worried us most. In the first innings we didn't think
Gomes or Logie was out and Clive spoke out about it. He felt
that the mistakes were too glaring not to be commented on and
he said that if he never saw those two umpires again he won't be
unhappy.

For the rest, Kapil Dev maintained stoutly that he had been right to
ask the West Indies to bat first, although he admitted that his bowlers
failed to exploit the assistance in the wicket. But the West Indies
prepared to go to Bombay two up in the series. On the way they
continued to make mincemeat of India in the one-day internationals.
It began to look as though India's victory at Lords a few months
earlier had been a monumental aberration.

Richards went to Bombay determined to get among the runs:

Midway through a series, you know, it's time to find some kind
of form. You've had all the zone games and all the other minor
fixtures and by the time the third test comes up, if you're going
to do well, it's about time. I was not going into the test match in
any particular frame of mind. But obviously I wanted to try and
get a big score.

The evening before the test match a number of friends gathered in
his hotel room to talk about the prospects for the game and to wish
him the best of luck. It was extraordinary how many bona fide
supporters of the Indian team were slapping Richards on the back
and expressing the hope that they would be privileged to see him
make a hundred. The phone rang constantly. Gavaskar's sister-in-
law called to express her good wishes. An Indian film producer, who
had somehow found his way into the room, insisted that Richards
should speak to a leading Indian film star. He also wanted to see
Richards make a century in Bombay. To add to it all, there was also

173

some talk that the Prime Minister of Antigua, Lester Bird, might travel to Bombay from Delhi where he was attending the 1983 Commonwealth Prime Ministers' Conference.

India won the toss and this time Kapil Dev decided to have first use of the wicket. Vengsarkar made a fine century, but India's innings lost its momentum on the second day and an entire day's play was spent in making 171 runs – and that by a team two down in a six-match series. From 259 for 4 they crawled pointlessly to 463. That score probably ensured that India would not lose the match, but it also meant that there was little chance of Kapil Dev pulling one test match back.

Instead of giving his bowlers the opportunity to have a go at the West Indies for an hour or so before stumps on the second day, Kapil Dev allowed his team's innings to run its full course and only six overs were possible against the West Indies before play ended. Haynes and Greenidge negotiated those with some discomfort because the ball had begun to turn.

On the third day of the Bombay test Greenidge was out for 13 just on the stroke of lunch. His 13 runs had taken him just under two hours. Richie Richardson, playing in his first test, was sent in ahead of his compatriot Viv Richards and was immediately on his way back into the pavilion for nought. He was adjudged leg-before, although he insisted that he had played the ball. It was a sad start to test cricket for the promising Antiguan, but he let in the man enthusiastic crowds are fond of calling 'King Richards'.

His first scoring shot was a powerful on drive to the boundary fence. His next was a chip to mid-wicket, flicked so effortlessly that it was with some surprise that the crowd saw the ball racing to the boundary well out of the reach of the chasing Indian fielder. Andy Roberts maintains that Richards is the only batsman to play that shot to such perfection. From the moment he applied his wrists to the shot, there were shouts of approval from his West Indian team-mates.

Before Richards came to the crease the West Indian scoring had been slow. Now the pace was getting better. He hit Binny over mid-on for 4, swept Ravi Shastri down to deep backward square and then lifted Binny over long-on for another boundary. He deftly picked the gaps in the field, and always seemed to find enough space to steer the ball away from Kapil Dev's men.

The 50 partnership came in just under 40 minutes. After tea, and with Prime Minister Lester Bird watching his countryman from the President's box, Richards sent a half-volley sailing into one of the stands of the Bombay Cricketground. He had a great stroke of luck before he reached his fifty. He failed to get hold of a ball from Ravi Shastri intending to hit it over mid-wicket, but Kapil Dev just could not keep it within his grasp.

'I was terrified,' he said later, 'I felt my heart beating so loudly. I thought to myself: "Not again. Having got into the forties, I shall fail again." Then I looked around and realised that Kapil just couldn't hold the ball. God I was relieved.'

From then on Richards could not be denied. His innings never reached the classic mould of some other performances, but by the time he reached 70, even though the Indian spinners were turning the ball, his century looked assured. He went to 77, hitting Mahinder over long-off for six, and in the next over raced through the eighties with three boundaries. His century came after 193 minutes, off 131 balls.

The Antiguan Prime Minister led the applause. As the sound of firecrackers reverberated round the ground, Richards raised his bat above his head in a gesture of genuine relief. He had struggled on the tour, failed, and now he had triumphed. Undefeated at close of play, he was applauded all the way into the pavilion. The West Indies ended the third day with their score on 204 for 3, Richards 103 not out; his fifteenth test century.

It was left to the West Indies team manager, Wes Hall, to inform Richards how his innings had been given the seal of approval by Antigua's Prime Minister. Mr Bird had been forced to leave Bombay before the close of play to return to the deliberations of the Commonwealth Prime Ministers in Delhi. But Hall reported that the Prime Minister had been confident that Richards would get his hundred and had treated the rest of the small official gathering to a running commentary on the art of batting according to King Richards. He also showed his appreciation in a more tangible way: just before the team boarded the bus to return to the Taj Hotel, Wes Hall pressed into Richards' hands a hundred-dollar note which had come from the Prime Minister with the instructions that Viv was to 'buy a few drinks for the rest of the boys in celebration'. Richards smiled approvingly.

In the lobby of the team hotel a small knot of young cricket enthusiasts and their fathers, mothers and uncles converged on

Richards, some wanting autographs, others merely content to shake him warmly by the hand. His hotel room was hardly much quieter. The phone rang incessantly. From all over the country people were ringing to congratulate Viv Richards for having ended his run of indifferent form in Bombay. One woman called up to say that his high score had been a certainty from the moment she had decided to remember him in her prayers the night before. Richards thanked her with the marked politeness he accords all callers and encouraged her to continue praying.

Recounting the highlights of his innings, he said he had been surprised about the extent to which the ball had turned and bounced. And on the couple of occasions when he came close to getting out, his miscues had been brought on by the turning ball. 'A couple of times there I thought I was really gone, man. My heart was really in my mouth,' he said.

He managed only 20 more runs on the following day, before the turn and bounce finally had the better of him. Inching out of his ground to smother the spin, he discovered too late that the ball was not there to be hit. It was a quicker one, which also spun sharply away to off, leaving wicket-keeper Kirmani with the relatively simple job of taking off the bails.

Richards, other century on the 1983 Indian tour came in the fourth one-day international, just before the West Indies convincingly won the six-test series by going three up in the fifth test.

As the West Indies overwhelmed India by 104 runs, he scored 149 glorious runs, batting with the freedom and thunderous form of a man free from earlier concerns about failure. The West Indies run chase had suffered an early setback when Desmond Haynes was out for one, but Richards and Greenidge put on 221 runs for the second wicket, scoring at just over seven runs per over throughout. It was a memorable display of attacking cricket which had even the partisan Indian crowd chanting the names of their West Indian heroes. Richards' 149 came off 99 balls and included three sixes and twenty fours. No less aggressive was Gordon Greenidge who hit five sixes and ten fours off only 94 deliveries.

After that the West Indies completed the rout in the penultimate test, clinching victory in the series by dismissing India for 90 in their second innings. It was India's lowest total in 53 tests against the West Indies. The hero of that game was the West Indies captain, Clive Lloyd, who in his farewell test series in India gave Kapil Dev and his bowlers the hiding of their lives. At the end of the West Indies second innings he was not out with 161. Time and time again, the Indian bowlers thought they had broken the back of the West Indies batting, only to see the tall powerful figure of Lloyd emerge from the pavilion, with his long loping walk to the middle. Perhaps the best player of spin in the West Indies side, Lloyd 's average when the West Indies took the series was just over 92. And that from a thirty-nine-year-old who was thinking throughout that 1983 tour of giving up West Indies test cricket and the captaincy to make way for a younger man. Richards' admiration for Clive Lloyd is boundless.

He has always given the spinners in India a hard time. He uses his height well, gets well down the track to kill the spin and is probably the best sweeper to leg in the game. And of course anything short, Lloydie hits them out of the ground. He is such a powerful hitter of the ball. He's had a sensational tour. To average over 90 in five test matches is no joke. Really one of the great players of our time, really. We're just lucky to have him on our side. Talk about leading by example. You couldn't find a captain who did more for the team with the bat than he's done on this tour.

After five tests Richards was fifth in the team's batting averages with just over 34. The pressure of international cricket competitions today, he believes, makes it impossible for any batsman to be top scorer in his side in every tournament. As an illustration, Richards cites the West Indies playing programme in 1983–84.

The players do not complain too loudly because continuous cricket is one way of ensuring that players get decent wages for their efforts. It is also a result of the 'Kerry Packer revolution'.

Having played the Prudential World Cup in England in the summer of 1983, West Indies went to India for six test matches, six three-day games, one two-day match and five one-day internationals.

In early January a tough programme of one-day matches (some day/night fixtures) began in Australia. The West Indies, along with Australia and Pakistan began the Benson and Hedges World Series Cup in Melbourne on 8 January when the West Indies played Australia. Two days later Australia met Pakistan in Sydney, and the tournament ended with three finals, the last of which was a highly controversial one because the West Indies felt they had taken the trophy by winning the first two.

From Australia, the players flew home to the West Indies for a test series against the Australians beginning at the end of February. This went on right up to the start of the English season when the West Indies came to England for a five-match test series. Richard says:

You've got to be very fit and tough for this kind of schedule, but it's your job. We're paid to play cricket and that's what we must do. But you do get jaded and stale. It's bound to happen. No one can keep on like that without feeling some effects. But you conserve your energies and do your best to minimise the bad effects. I get tired. But even more important is to try not to get injured. You see, some injuries can come just from over-extending yourself. But it's all part of the modern game and that's the way we must play now.

CHAPTER TWELVE

As a man and a cricketer his future seems
gold-lined which is ... why people look that
much harder for chinks
                David Gower about Viv Richards
                                        1983

If Richards had any way of marking out his own 'gold-lined' future, the first stage along the way would be the leadership of the West Indies team. Antiguans certainly believe that the job should be his by right. He has thought about it a great deal and has formulated his own clear philosophy about what the job entails.

> I see the role of captain as acting in such a way that you get the best out of all the players on your team. That obviously means knowing all the players, what they are good at and what their weaknesses are, but it also means having a good rapport with the players. A captain must be very open to suggestions from play-ers. He must be big enough to accept those without feeling that his position is in any way diminished or threatened by giving others players their head. At various stages of a game, players might come up to you with suggestions, saying: 'I think if we do this we've got a chance'. A captain must assess these and act accordingly. Of course, the good captain must always appreciate that the buck stops with him. It is, in the end, his responsibility.
>
> I do not think that this kind of responsibility affects my batting or my play generally. I have been a very responsible captain of Somerset for part of the 1983 season and that in itself did not affect my cricket in any adverse way. But the good captain does not sacrifice other guys. If there is a problem, as captain you think that you put yourself up first to try and solve it, not do it by sacrificing another player. If a captain were to sacrifice others when difficulties arise, that would make him a less confident person and a less sufficient player.

His team-mates question whether Richards has the right temperament to captain
the West Indies

The Richards 'temperament' – his tendency still, in moments of the
most agonising pressure, to fly off the handle – will be a deciding
factor about how long he leads the West Indies. Another problem
might well be his pride. His team-mates in the West Indies team talk
about his aristocratic air: the manner of his walk to the wicket; the
way he plays the game, hardly ever tailoring his natural aggression to
conditions in which lesser men would plod around and play with the
utmost care and defence. But knowing you are probably the best
batsman alive puts enormous strain on a player.

He is also slightly impatient of any excessive show of authority and
would have a testing time with the West Indies cricket establishment.
But, with understanding, the authorities who manage the game in
Port of Spain and in Kingston would find Viv Richards a thoughtful
captain, a man who reads the game well and who demonstrates a
shrewd appreciation of strategy. He has also discovered that he is
very good at motivating other players, although that quality might
not be needed among the older hands in the West Indies cricket
squad. He'll certainly be an inspiration to the younger West Indies
players. Eldine Ashworth Elderfield Baptiste, who is a fellow Antiguan, makes the point clearly.

180

'Vivian Richards has been my inspiration,' he says. 'He gave me a lot of comforting and encouraging words when I went down with injury problems halfway through an English season. I think it was one of the main reasons why although I missed a lot of matches I still returned reasonable figures at the end of the season: 800 runs and just over 50 wickets. It's so good to have people who can help you in the way Viv helped me.'

There are many similar stories from Somerset players about Richards willing his side on to match-winning performances with dressing-room pep-talks.

When he deputised for Ian Botham for a part of Somerset's 1983 season he put himself lower down in the batting order to give an opportunity to some of the younger club players to establish themselves by settling down to playing knocks for their side. He is very good, too, at talking to younger players about the contemporary test cricketers he has known. Viv Richards talks most enthusiastically about Ian Botham, Clive Lloyd, David Gower and Andy Roberts.

Ian Botham is a personal friend. I admire him a lot as a man who is very down-to-earth and who stands up for his rights. [It is possible that this latter is one of the facets of the Botham personality which Richards most respects.]

What I like about him is that he seems to have the same lifestyle and approach to the game that West Indians have. If Ian Botham comes to the wicket and his side is in trouble, as he did when England won that famous test match against Australia a few seasons ago [1981], his first instinct is to attack. That is the kind of thing the West Indian does. Sometimes we become unstuck and so does Ian, but that's the aggressive way he plays the game. All credit to him.

Ian also speaks his mind. He is down-to-earth and frank. He's taken a great deal of criticism for doing that, but he says what he thinks. I like that. He responds to criticism, he's human, he's not a plastic guy.

The main point about his play is that he plays cricket the way people like to see the game played. Ian Botham is with the public's thinking about cricket and you better believe it. They need the spirit and the enthusiasm he brings to the game. On his day, playing well, he is magnificent. There is never a dull moment when he's batting. People will tell you that he plays

181

rash shots, but that's part of the game he plays. He will take any attack apart when he is on his day.

Ian has the ability to be a class batsman, but he believes that there is probably something equally important or perhaps even more important. He is an entertainer.

Not a lot of people would believe this, but we don't try to outdo each other if we're batting at the same time for Somerset. I think that's a kind of fiction in people's mind, you see. They think, here's Ian Botham, one of the most dashing batsmen in cricket, and Viv Richards, who can also hit the ball a bit, this must be explosive because they'll try to outdo each other and it will be great. But that never really happens, you can't actually play cricket like that. I certainly never try to outdo Ian – he is so powerful a player.

And Ian showed in the Nat West Trophy semi-final, he can play a patient innings and hold things together if he is needed to. That innings at the Oval [1983] was a very mature one, when a lot of other people would have thought we would have no chance. So he can restrain himself.

He is a good bowler. He varies his pace, his deliveries, he gets the ball to move about off the seam and in the air and is constantly keeping the batsmen guessing. But the most remarkable thing about Ian's cricket is his sheer aggression, his enthusiasm for the game. I think I am very fortunate that he thinks of me as a friend and as someone he can confide in. He is the greatest. Cricket will never be dull when Ian's playing.

It is perhaps not entirely surprising to learn that Ian Botham repays the compliment. He goes further. He advances the theory that Viv Richards is as good a batsman as the great Don Bradman. He believes that the manner in which modern cricket is played, with all its attendant pressures and skill of field placings, means that contemporary players must show greater skill far more consistently if they are to be classed among the best in the world.

Richards has never been drawn into the argument, and whatever he believes about its inherent merit remains unstated.

He is much more forthcoming on the merits and the class of the Guyanese and West Indies star Clive Lloyd.

OPPOSITE Ian Botham – 'his first instinct is to attack' (ASP)

I think Clive Lloyd is one of the greatest players in the game and has been repeatedly proved as such. My most strong memories of his ability was watching him bat during my first tour of India. It was my first overseas tour for the West Indies and I was naturally nervous, worried about doing well and perplexed by the guiles of the Indian spin bowlers. I stood at the other end and watched Lloydie master those guys. It was the most amazing performance I've ever seen. Anything well-up was driven firmly. If ever he was in doubt, he reached well down the wicket to kill the spin. Anything short he cut or drove off the back foot or hooked for four. Half-volleys he murdered. And his sweeps to the leg-side are the best of those around.

As captain, Clive is quite laid back. He knows that there are players who know what's required of them and those who must be assisted. He has 'read' a succession of West Indian players well and he knows how to deal with them. As a captain he's come in for his fair share of criticism, but I don't think it's ever worried him too much. During the 1983 Indian tour Clive was quite outspoken about some of the umpiring. Some people felt that he had acted wrongly. But he pointed out that he had been trying all along to control things and not have a repeat of that New Zealand tour when the West Indian players were criticised for kicking down stumps and so on when their appeals went unheard. He's been a great captain and the side under him has won the biggest honours in the game.

Of the England players, Viv Richards believes that Leicestershire's David Gower is perhaps one of the best batsmen.

David Gower is sheer class. He is without doubt one of the best timers of the cricket ball I've seen. I feel sure that he is being looked as an England captain of the future and there's no reason why he shouldn't be a great success. Gower is the difference between players of average ability and those of exceptional pedigree. He has time to play his shots and he strokes the ball beautifully.

He is really sensational to watch on his day. He can light up the park with his play, you know. He's made some marvellous runs against the West Indies. Our quick bowlers always make

OPPOSITE David Gower – 'sheer class' (*Adrian Murrell*)

all batsmen fight for their runs and batsmen who are not afraid of the challenge, as Gower, always make our quickies get their tails up. But it's wonderful to see Gower doing battle with some West Indian pace on a good wicket. It's one of cricket's finest sights.

I feel sure that he's been groomed for the job of guiding the fortunes of the England team of the future and he seems to get on well with players. He goes for his shots, he too plays with a kind of West Indian flair and grace and he's exciting. The players seem to regard him well and he has a sound future in the game.

Richards has met the best fast bowlers of his time and he still feels that his compatriot Andy Roberts is on his day among the best in the world. But he has also been forced to learn the hard way that Australian quick bowlers are among the most aggressive and attacking in the world.

Andy Roberts thinks about the game and about his bowling. He schemes to get the batsmen out. If you talk to him, you realise that he knows the weaknesses of individual players, so that he knows how they could be prised out. He knows those people who like to clip them on the onside; Andy bowls outswingers to them. He attacks their off-stump. He's really a great thinker. He's learnt a lot about quick bowling and uses his head all the time.

The great difference about Australian pace bowlers is the manner in which they attack you. Those guys are the toughest to play cricket against. They'll try to knock you down while you're batting and if you manage to score a few runs against them, particularly if you hit them for four or so, they get so mad and they'll abuse you, you know verbal abuse and curse you and so on. If you're confident, you survive, if not, Lillee and Thomson and guys like Pascoe will terrify you out of the game. They are really the toughest competitors.

I remember the first time I played against those guys we tried to take the attack to them. It didn't work and on quick wickets they ran all over us. It's the Australian way of playing cricket. Perhaps they've never forgotten the battles against England in the old bodyline days and decided never to be subjected to that kind of thing again. These days they are the aggressors.

Andy Roberts – the thinking cricketer's bowler *(Adrian Murrell)*

On the Indian tour of 1983 Viv Richards had an excellent opportunity to study at close quarters the talents of the new Indian captain Kapil Dev. West Indian players tend to be very cautious in their assessment of Kapil for fear that they might be accused of a slight prejudice arising out of India's Prudential World Cup Victory. Viv Richards tends to be characteristically generous while pointing out that perhaps the talents of the Indian captain have been a little overestimated.

The great thing about Kapil Dev is that he gets on with the job. Leading an Indian team in India, in the full heat of all the criticisms which come from so many quarters, because everyone has such high expectations of the team, is not an easy job. Kapil

187

manages to put all that aside and gets on with the business of playing cricket. He could so easily get involved in the politics of the Indian game.

When he played against us before, in the West Indies and in the World Cup, he's showed himself an excellent attacking bowler. He is an intelligent bowler and his best delivery is the one which he manages to make go away from the batsman at the very last second. It's a beautiful outswinger with which he's picked up quite a few wickets. India's problem tends to be that no other bowler at the moment has the speed of Kapil and so he tends to be rather on his own. Madan Lal and these other guys are not of his pace.

On this tour his batting has been a bit fragile. And I'm not very sure whether true class is there. Maybe it's the responsibility of leading a team under pressure, playing at home, but he's been got out for quite a few low scores on the 1983 tour and he never really threatened to dominate the West Indies attack with a big score. Like the other Indian batsmen, he's susceptible to speed. Sometimes there's a gap between bat and pad. He can be a good fielder. But the main thing is, whatever you say about Kapil, one should remember that he still has a great deal of cricket to play and will improve. He can become a really good player.

We hope he is not too affected by the fact that India under his captaincy have been totally humiliated by us on this (the 1983) tour. Cricket here is taken very seriously and politics gets into it. Already they have been talking about India's poor showing in the Indian parliament, and when that happens somebody's head could roll. But India under Kapil have just come up against a very good West Indies team and all the blame for India's defeat in this series cannot be put at the door of Kapil Dev alone.

Of the many West Indies 'stars' of the future, Viv Richards thinks that the West Indies wicket-keeper Jeff Dujon and the young Antiguan quick bowler Ferris are the ones to watch.

I have captained teams in which young Ferris has played and there is no doubt that he seems to be another in the long tradition

OPPOSITE Kapil Dev – perhaps the best is yet to come (*Adrian Murrell*)

of West Indies quick bowlers. He's a strong boy, tall, just over six foot, and he's quick. He does deliver the ball with a great deal of speed. Under the guidance of Andy Roberts he's been picking up all the other fine points of the fast bowler's craft, and I'm sure he'll do well. It would be great to see him playing for the West Indies which I'm sure he'll do. They like fast bowlers in the West Indies. Our current team is really built around the quickies. They do the damage, and guys like Larry Gomes and I have not had to be called on a great deal when you have Marshall, Davis and Andy and Mickey Holding around. So a young guy like Ferris has something to aspire to. If he manages to get into that company he should have the confidence to go on and to do well.

Jeff Dujon is perhaps *the* West Indies batsman of the future. He's a magnificent player, and he strikes the ball really beautifully. You can't say that of many players. His square driving is something to see. He plays well off the back foot, on drives well, but his greatest asset is that he uses his feet to the spinners. That's particularly useful in India where you come up against so many spinners. He also has the right temperament.

It is possible that he should bat a little higher up in the West Indies order. Maybe his natural place should be above that of Larry Gomes. At the moment he bats 6 or 7. That's perhaps a little too low down for a batter of Dujon's potential. There's also been the discussion about whether his wicket-keeping has taken away from his batting. It's not always easy to make that kind of judgment.

The West Indies have had good wicket-keeper batsmen, but some of the best gave up. Clyde Walcott gave up and so did Rohan Kanhai. Dujon has scored well for the West Indies, but his real run-scoring potential is yet to come. He still gets dismissed far too many times just when he's well in and should have gone on to make hundreds. But they'll come, I'm sure. He is definitely the man to watch in the West Indies team of the future. He is also captain of Jamaica so he has some leadership qualities.

He's got some marvellous runs on this 1983 Indian tour. His 98 in the test match in Ahmadabad had all the Indian sports-

OPPOSITE Jeff Dujon – the West Indies batting star of the future *(Adrian Murrell)*

writers wondering whether a score of 98 could ever be as good as a century and they decided that Dujon's batting that day was as good as any hundred. The commentators talked about how he managed to conquer the problems of a very difficult wicket, to stay with the tail-enders and help lay the foundation for what turned out to be a very important West Indies win and a turning-point for us in the series. He makes batting look pretty uncomplicated and has a full range of pretty classy strokes. People will see a lot of him in the years to come.

Of the Pakistani players, the names Imran Khan and Zaheer Abass come most readily to Viv Richards' lips.

There isn't a better way of showing the influence Imran has on a Pakistan test team than by thinking how much they missed him in Australia in 1983. They were totally outclassed because they didn't have the one man who can turn their fortunes round with bat and ball. There's no doubt about it, he's a great all-rounder.

He is also a captain who leads by example. He communicates his enthusiasm for the game to his players. His bowling is tremendous. He's fast, genuinely fast, he can move the ball about and he has a good yorker which is a devastating ball. Imran can bowl out a side. He's had some great figures in English county cricket and even more memorable performances for his country. That's the real stamp of a great player – there's always something happening when he's in the thick of the action, you know, there's never a dull moment. He's had this bad injury to his leg during the 1983 season. I hope it mends quickly and if it does we will continue to see a great deal more of him. You know, he's a very aristocratic guy. He makes his presence felt on a team.

Zaheer Abass is one of the great onside players in the game as he is capable of making a large number of runs. But it's very strange that he hasn't made as many big scores for Pakistan as he has playing in county cricket in England. I don't know why that is, but he is a sound batsman, hits the ball well and stylishly and when he's in form he will dominate any attack. But he's never really put together all those double centuries he's got for Gloucestershire for Pakistan.

Viv Richards admits that cricket has affected the constancy of his family life. During an English summer, it is only possible for him to go home to his wife Miriam and his two children when fixtures are played at home or very near home. And when he goes to India, Australia, Pakistan and New Zealand, he has never found it possible to have his family travel with him. These long absences from home bring their difficulties. When the West Indies team plays at home things are a little better: Miriam and the children are usually in Antigua before Christmas and for the succeeding three months of the West Indies tour, before it's back to England for the following summer.

> All this makes life a little difficult. It's very hard on families and it's tough on Miriam. She gets very lonely. It's tough in England, a little better in Antigua because there Miriam and the kids are with their own folk. It makes a great deal of difference. I think Miriam is quite resigned to her life of loneliness from my absences, she's quite understanding. She realises that in this game you've got to be away from home for a great deal of the time. Antigua is still home for both of us. England is our second home.

Although she enjoys the trappings of success which Viv's cricket has brought to her life, with homes in Taunton and Antigua, life without her husband for so much of the year is very lonely. Miriam is a quiet girl who has made few friends in England, and who therefore spends a great deal of time on her own caring for her two young children.

Some of her best friends are the wives of other senior West Indian players, and they are often the only people to whom she can talk when Viv is abroad for many months at a time. Tours in the West Indies, when she too can see her friends at home and spend a greater proportion of her evenings with Viv, are the high points in her year.

The family unit is of great importance to Richards: he is intensely loyal to his wife and children and to his brother and parents in the West Indies. His parents have been a great stabilising force in his life and he feels it's part of his duty to ensure that they share in his success. Deep down, there is perhaps the feeling that he is making a celebrated career in a game in which his father only just failed to become a famous name.

Viv Richards enjoys the trappings of success his cricket has brought – not in a particularly ostentatious manner, but more with reflective quiet satisfaction and pride. Cricket in England affords him little time to do a great deal other than listen to his favourite reggae and calypso music and watch films on video. Life in Antigua could be a little more grand: 'I have this friend at home who owns a big sea-going yacht and it's marvellous to go out sailing or fishing for a couple of days. It's wonderful to be able to get away from it all like that. That is really very enjoyable.'

Back in England, he gets involved in more predictable things. One day last summer he sat in the office of his friend Peter McCoombe discussing how it would be logistically possible for him to take part in a television competition for Superstars in the Far East and appear at a function in Birmingham in England a couple of days later. It was not going to be easy since he hates flying. In the end he insisted on not missing Birmingham, not only because the thought of going to the Far East and back inside a week seemed a terrifying proposition, but also because he'd been asked to appear in Birmingham by a pop group of young Jamaican kids whose reggae hit record had just gone to number one in the British charts. The group had particularly requested an appearance by Viv Richards and he didn't want to miss it or to disappoint them. He gives you the impression that he takes his social responsibilities seriously, as he does his cricket.

For someone who claims to be apolitical, Richards spends a great deal of time talking about 'political' subjects. And he is increasingly equivocal on the question of whether he would consider a political career back in Antigua when his playing days come to an end. There would certainly be a great deal of pressure in Antigua for him to do so eventually, and he admits that, from wanting no part of it, he's begun to rethink his attitude to politics: 'I thought I had made a firm decision about that. But I'm not so sure. The main thing is can someone who's in charge be honest? Honesty should be the main point of politics. I've discovered that there are some politicians who do try to work for the people. It is possible. And I think I would have to give the matter a second thought.'

Although he keeps well clear of any political involvement at the moment, and shuns political controversy, Richards is in fact deeply interested in the course of West Indian politics as it affects the region.

His political philosophy is still unformed, but he's something of an idealist. He believes that it should be possible to order a society

OPPOSITE Relaxing with Miriam and Matara

with something of the perfection he attempts to bring to his cricket.

He was deeply affected by his meeting and his later friendship with the former Grenadian leader Maurice Bishop, who was killed in a bloody attempted coup on the island in October 1983. The first meeting of the two men was totally devoid of any political interest and was concerned strictly with cricket. For years the Grenadians had been trying to get their island listed as a recognised venue for international cricket and Viv Richards was involved in trying to help that come about.

There was an immediate rapport between politician and cricketer. The admiration was mutual. Bishop took a liking to Viv Richards who had come from a tiny island just like Grenada and had risen to international prominence in sport. In his turn, Richards fell under the spell of a young, brilliant, idealistic politician, who was trying to forge new alliances for his country in the interest of its development and the advancement of its people. They became friends.

In so far as Bishop preached black pride and socialism, he may have provided a kind of intellectual reference for Richards' views. He saw Grenada as the focal point of a home-grown revolution which gave a certain status to people in one small part of the third world.

Viv Richards was deeply saddened by the death of Maurice Bishop and annoyed at the American intervention and by what he saw as the complicity of some other Caribbean countries, notably Barbados, in bringing about that intervention. He saw the presence of the American marines as a backward step for the Caribbean. He also feels he knows the origin of what he calls the 'bad feeling' between Grenada and Barbados, which culminated in the Barbadian Prime Minister asking the Americans to help restore order in Grenada:

> It all began because Maurice [Bishop] called Tom Adams [the Prime Minister of Barbados] a 'yard fowl' [a derogatory West Indian term of abuse for someone considered less worthy than a chicken which roams around in backyards finding its own food]. From that moment on there was enmity between the two men and Barbados was out to get the Bishop government. Asking the Americans to go in was Tom Adams' way of getting back at Maurice.

That's as far as Viv Richards would go on political matters. But he needn't go very much further at the moment – there are still too many runs to make for the West Indies on cricket grounds in Eng-

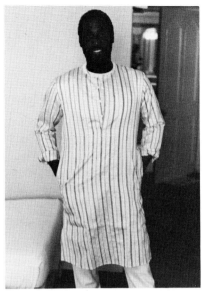
An impressive ambassador for his colour and his country

land, India, Pakistan, Australia and, of course, in the West Indies.

But Richards' friend and room-mate Ian Botham has always found him a good listener and a useful sounding-board for discussions about resolving career problems. Maybe that talent could find a useful niche in West Indian politics? And it is interesting to note that West Indian cricketers going into politics at the end of their careers is not without precedent in the region: the former fast bowler Wes Hall is now a respected senator in Barbados.

And perhaps Peter Roebuck is right.

Richards has the presence, the personality and the discretion to emerge as an impressive and weighty ambassador for his colour and for his country.

INDEX

Page numbers in *italic* refer to the illustrations

Pont, Keith, 117, 118–19
Proctor, 62

Rae, Allan, 108, 109–12
Raja, Wasin, 161
Rhamadhin, Sonny, 23, 24, 31
Richards, Gretel (mother), 32, 39, 48, 54–5, 193; *34*
Richards, Malcolm (father), 32, 39–40, 48, 54–5, 60, 193; *33, 34*
Richards, Matara (daughter), 130; *131, 195*
Richards, Mervyn (brother), *34*
Richards, Miriam (wife), 56, 57, 146, 193; *57, 147, 195*
Richardson, Richie, 174
Ring, 25
Robbins, Derek, 49, 61
Roberts, Andy, 3, 9, 11, 39, 47–8, 51, 55, 75, 81–3, 87, 88, 116, 152, 154, 155, 174, 181, 186, 190; *52, 187*
Roebuck, Peter, 18, 56–7, 102, 103–5, 117, 118, 119, 130, 134, 198; *58*
Rose, B.C., 103, 118, 135; *117*
Rowe, 140

Sandhu, 151, 152
Scotland, 131
Selvey, Mike, 14
Sharma, Yashpal, 151, 154, 155
Shastri, Ravi, 151–2, 172, 174, 175
Sidhu, 172
Simpson, Bobby, 12
Slocombe, Phil, 116, 118
Smith, N., 118–19
Snow, John, 10, 12
Sobers, Gary, 2, 14, 27, 30, 42, 91–6, 99, 108, 167
Solkar, 69

Statham, 83
Steele, David, 10
Steele, Ray, 109
Stollmeyer, Jeffrey, 25, 27, 28–9, 108, 110, 111
Stovold, 161
Swanton, Jim, 49, 68

Taylor, 118
Test and County Cricket Board (TCCB), 5, 108–10
Thomson, Jeff, 81, 138, 144, 186
Trueman, Freddie, 83
Turner, S., 118–19

Umrigar, Polly, 25
Underwood, Derek, 3, 10, 12, 14, 49, 53, 117

Valentine, Alfred, 23, 24
Vengsarkar, D.B., 87–8, 167, 174
Venkat, S., 85, 88, 152
Venkataraghavan, 152
Viswanath, G.R., 86, 88

Walcott, Clyde, 5–6, 23, 25–30, 95, 108, 167, 190
Webster, W.H., 109
Weekes, Everton, 23, 25–30, 85, 167
Wellard, Arthur, 159
West Indian Cricket Board, 22–30, 79, 106, 107, 108, 109–11, 115–16, 134–5
Williams, Eric, 15, 68
Willis, Bob, 12, 14, 144–5, 155
Wood, Barry, 65
Woolmer, 10
World Series Cricket, 107, 108–16
Worrell, Frank, 2, 16–18, 22, 23–4, 25–30, 59, 79, 81, 96, 107–8, 135, 167; *26*